Better Homes and Gardens

The secrets of
Good Gardening

An A–Z Guide

MURDOCH BOOKS
Sydney • London • Vancouver

Contents

A–Z guide to good gardening   4–127

Special features

Soil isn't just dirt   6

Watering and saving water   16

Gardening in containers   26

Planting   38

Pottering in a greenhouse   50

Out of season   54

You can't garden without tools   60

Lawns without tears   64

Propagation   78

Pruning   90

Garden safety   106

Winning the war against weeds 118

The joys of exhibiting   124

New topics are introduced with bold type.
Capitalised words denote separate entries.

ACID AND ALKALINE

One of the most important things to know about your soil is whether it is acid, alkaline or neutral, that is, balanced between the two states. An acid soil is one that contains little LIME (that is, compounds of calcium), an alkaline one has a lot of it; in a neutral soil, the lime is in balance with other elements. CALCIUM affects the availability of other nutrient elements, especially IRON,

which may be in severe shortage in a strongly alkaline soil. Some plants cannot cope with this — they will show symptoms of CHLOROSIS — and need to be grown in an acid soil; others like lime and prefer their soil alkaline.

The ideal is probably for the soil to be a little on the acid side of neutral, which will suit most plants, and you can give a little lime to those plants that need it — you might like to group them together. It is harder to make an alkaline soil acid; try mulching with organic matter (pine needles, though they take a long time to decay, are especially useful, being acid in themselves), and the desperate can try sprinkling sulphur on the soil which, as it weathers, will make the soil water acid and lock up some of the free calcium as insoluble calcium sulphate. Sulphur will, however, kill micro-organisms in the soil. This is not good, and if you garden on an alkaline soil and want to grow lime-hating plants your best course may be to grow them in containers or raised beds of lime-free

soil. Water them only with rain water, because where the soil is alkaline, the tap water almost certainly will be alkaline as well.

It is a general, though by no means hard and fast, rule that soils in humid coastal climates tend to be acid, those in drier inland climates alkaline.

The acidity/alkalinity of soil can be quantified precisely on the pH SCALE, where, on a scale of 1 to 14, 7 represents exact neutrality, anything less is acid, anything more is alkaline. Testing kits can be bought to measure pH. But it is easier to wait until Christmas to see what colour your local hydrangeas are: they will be blue in acid soils, pink in alkaline — if they can't seem to make up their minds then the soil is neutral. If you can't wait until then, try the old trick of putting a bit of soil on your tongue: limey soil tastes vaguely sweet, acid soil sour.

Lime-hating plants
Azaleas
Camellias
Rhododendrons
Many natives
Gardenias
Daphne odora
Kalmia latifolia
Luculia
Almost all lilies
Orchids

Lime-loving plants
Cabbages and their tribe
Bearded irises
Peonies
Carnations
Oriental poppies
Stocks
Foxgloves
Roses (though they will grow perfectly happily in a neutral or just slightly acid soil)

The same hydrangea that flowers clear pink in alkaline soil will be unmistakably blue in acid. (Though it will probably look lilac-tinted in a photograph.)

ADVICE AND HELP

No one ever gets to know everything there is to know about gardening, but there are various places to turn to for assistance.

Books are available on every aspect of horticulture, from the most basic to the most esoteric, and every gardener soon builds up a modest library of favourites. Two things to look out for: the most expensive aren't necessarily the best, and in interpreting the many excellent British and American books, don't forget that the Northern Hemisphere seasons don't translate exactly to Australia — June in Britain is more likely to be equivalent to our October, not December or January — that our sunny aspect is south, and that their major problem is apt to be frost and cold, ours heat and dryness.

Landscape architects and **garden designers** can be worth every penny of their fees if you are making a new garden or remodelling an old one.

Your local **nursery** staff should know a great deal about the best plants for your conditions, and how to grow them.

Your local **council** (try their Parks Department) or your state **Department of Agriculture** both have experts with local knowledge to offer.

Your **fellow gardeners** will also understand local conditions. These may be friends and neighbours or members of the local **garden club**.

And if what you need is someone to actually do a job, you will find **professional gardeners** advertising in the local paper; most of them will be happy to come in for the occasional few hours as needed. Check them out: ask for references, and don't be shy about asking just what their charges are.

AFRICAN VIOLETS

For all its popularity, the charming African violet (*Saintpaulia ionantha* in its many cultivars) is something of a prima donna, apt to sulk when its demands aren't met. If yours isn't performing, the chances are that it is displeased with one (or all) of three things:

Don't expect your African violets to look like this all the time; even when happy, most bloom in flushes rather than continuously.

- The room is **too dark** — move it into bright light, but not direct sun; a sunny window-sill shaded by a lace curtain will be about right.
- The atmosphere is **not humid enough** — try a bathroom or kitchen window-sill or standing the pot on (not in) a saucer full of damp gravel.
- It is suffering from **wet feet** — don't water until the surface soil in the pot is quite dry, and never leave the plant standing in a saucer full of water.

If it fails to bloom even in these conditions, it may just be a shy-flowering cultivar, and some are happier in a greenhouse.

In subtropical climates, with warm winters and humid summers, African violets will grow quite happily in a shaded place out of doors, either as potplants or in a bed of leafy soil. In Brisbane my mother had a rockery planted with them, to the envy of her friends.

AIR LAYERING

More than just a party trick — though it smacks of magic — air layering is a useful way to propagate shrubs that are reluctant to root from cuttings but are too stiffly branched to be bent down to the soil to be LAYERED in the ordinary way. You can also get a bigger plant to start with than can be made from a cutting. And it is easy to do.

AIR LAYERING

1 *Select a suitable branch, and cut partway through the stem, on a slant*

2 *Prop the cut open with a matchstick and brush with rooting hormone, reinforcing everything by tying it to something like a chopstick if needed.*

3 *Make a funnel of plastic (an old shopping bag will be fine) and pack with wet sphagnum moss; then tie up the top to hold all in place and keep it moist. When the roots push against the plastic, cut off the whole thing, remove plastic and plant.*

Soil isn't just dirt

I once had an acquaintance who was disinherited by his garden-minded (and wealthy) grandmother for referring to the soil of his new garden as 'dirt'. She had a point, for the soil is the foundation of life, and should be treated with respect. But then, so did he, for soil is indeed basically dirt, that is, rock that has been ground exceeding small by thousands and millions of years of erosion. To an extent, the type of rock from which the soil was derived influences its nature — limestone soils tend to be alkaline for instance — but more important is the size of the particles, which is the determining factor in the **structure** of the soil, and that is what plants are concerned with.

If the particles are greater than a couple of millimetres or so, we don't have soil but **gravel**; **sand** grains range from about 0.025 millimetres to about 1 millimetre, **silt** is in the order of a couple of thousandths of a millimetre, **clay** even less, sometimes much less, than that. None of these sizes are the kind that you can measure without laboratory equipment, and in any case most soils contain a mixture of sand, silt and clay. If they are present in balanced proportions, the result is **loam**; if they are mostly in the upper range of size, you have **sandy loam;** if mostly in the smallest sizes, a **clay loam.** Pure sand is rare, except near the beach; so is pure clay, of more use to potters and the owners of brickworks than to gardeners.

Determining how your soil is classified is easy enough. Just take a small handful when it is just moist, and make a ball with it in the palm of your hand. Now examine it. Does it feel gritty, and fall apart easily? You have a sandy soil. Does it feel gritty, but hold its shape? A sandy or light loam. Does it feel slightly sticky, hold its shape easily, but is easy to break up? Celebrate: you have the gardener's dream, a medium loam. If you can polish it with your fingers, then it is a clay or heavy loam; and if you can polish it and knead it into delicate shapes like potter's clay, then that is just what you have. The terms light and heavy don't refer to the actual weight of the soil, for sand is in fact heavier than clay, but to the ease with which you can dig it, as in 'light' or 'heavy' work.

If you dig deep enough, you'll find that below the topsoil lies the subsoil, which is usually the same type of soil as the topsoil, but a different colour, because it contains less humus (about which more later). Below that again, sometimes a very long way below, lies rock. Sometimes, as

Sloping banks can be a problem, as the soil will wash away. Groundcover plants will hold it in place, or you can build retaining walls. Tall walls need professional design and are expensive, but you can use a series of smaller ones to make terraces, as here. The walls are made from treated pine logs, and the manufacturers will have directions on how to make them. They look a bit raw at present, but the growth of plants will soon put them in their place.

TESTING SOIL STRUCTURE

1 *A ball of clay soil will hold its shape in your hand.*

2 *Sandy soil feels gritty, and will fall apart easily.*

3 *Loam will be crumbly, but won't fall apart entirely.*

in sandstone country, the rock is close to the surface, and sometimes the subsoil is so compact that it might as well be rock (when you can break it up by the laborious process of DOUBLE DIGGING). But as long as you have from 30 to 50 centimetres of soil before you hit rock or a concrete-solid subsoil, you needn't be too concerned.

DRAINAGE

While a medium loam topsoil is the ideal, as you can grow anything in it, don't worry if your soil is on the light or heavy side, as there are still plenty of things you can grow to perfection. True, most plants have their preferences, but few are really pernickety. Not about soil type, anyway. What is more important to most is **drainage,** the ability of the ground to shed excess water and not become waterlogged. Again, it's easy enough to check your drainage. Just dig a hole about 40 centimetres deep (as deep as you can take the spade comfortably) and fill it with water; if it is quite empty within 24 hours or so, your drainage is adequate. If it isn't, then you either need to concentrate on plants that like a wet soil — there are many, though lawn grass and most vegetables aren't among them — or take steps to improve matters. If the design of your garden suits them, you can build raised beds above the general soil level, or you can lay drainpipes. This is heavy work, but it's less of a skilled job in these days of plastic drainage pipes than it was when you had to carefully set out short lengths of terracotta. The plastic pipes come in long rolls, and you place them at the bottom of trenches about 40 to 50 centimetres deep, covering them over with gravel before filling in the soil again.

The problem is that you have to lead the water away somewhere. If your local council won't allow you to connect your system to the storm water system (most won't), and there are no convenient ditches or creeks downhill, you will be forced to make a sump at the lowest point of the property. Just dig a hole a metre or more (preferably more) deep and a metre or so wide and fill it with stones and rubble. You can plant thirsty plants next to it in the hope that they will lap up the excess. No need for willows; smaller things like cannas can do the job too. But make sure you're not discharging your excess water onto a neighbour's property — you won't be thanked for it. Fortunately, the need for this kind of work is relatively rare.

IMPROVING YOUR SOIL

You can adjust the balance of less than ideal soil by adding what it lacks — clay to sandy soils, sand to heavy ones — or by using various proprietary soil conditioners that agglomerate too-small particles together. But such things need to be added in large amounts to do much good, and it's easy to find yourself playing with truckloads — to say nothing of the hard, hard work of actually digging them in. A landscape contractor finds it easier, using trucks, equipment and strong-backed staff.

Much better to accept the soil you have, and gradually improve it by adding as much organic matter — compost, old manure, fallen leaves, grass clippings and what have you — as you can. Organic matter binds sandy soils and loosens

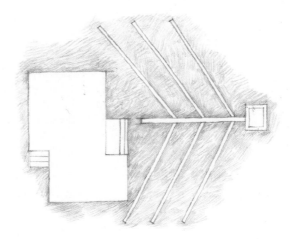

Laying out soil drain pipes, with branches leading to a main and thence to a sump, all falling (for preference) away from the house.

clay and eventually rots down to make **humus,** and it is humus that makes soil more than just dirt. Humus gives fertile soil its dark colour, and indeed, by supporting a multitude of living organisms from microbes to worms it transforms the soil into a living thing in its own right; the plants you cultivate are only part of its web of life. Plants can only take their nourishment in the form of inorganic substances dissolved in the soil moisture — the **soil solution** — and these can be replenished by artificial FERTILISERS, but in some way that science still doesn't properly understand, they need the assistance of humus itself and the micro-organisms it supports to flourish. It is only by adding organic matter that the humus supply can be replenished and the soil kept healthy, and the wise gardener considers the health of the soil above all else. That is why no properly managed garden can be without a COMPOST heap, and why you should be wary of chemicals in any form; they can poison the soil's micro-organisms.

Cultivating the soil, which means digging, loosens it and allows air into it. In the early stages of making a garden, you have a free hand and thorough, deep cultivation will pay dividends later. Once your permanent plantings are in place, you can't cultivate deeply and you use small forks, trowels and hoes to keep the surface loose (in **good tilth,** as gardeners say) so that it doesn't set into a crust that repels water and air. Set out the garden so that you aren't always walking on your beds, and thereby crushing the loose surface, to tend your plants. Beds shouldn't be more than about 3 metres wide if you can get at them from both sides, half that if they are accessible only from the front.

There is no need to be always digging in your compost; it can be laid on top as MULCH and the worms and other creatures will take the humus down where it is needed. Mulching can save work as well as being good for the plants.

It is possible to get obsessive about the details of your soil, but don't. As long as your drainage is sufficient, you keep the humus supply up, and you cultivate the surface occasionally, your soil will be healthy and you will have a flourishing garden.

For many years, air layering was the standard method of propagating rhododendrons, but it can be done with most plants. And it is a good way of dealing with that over-tall rubber tree in the office: create a new plant from the top half-metre or so, and when it is ready, discard the old plant and give the new one its pot.

ALKALINE
see ACID AND ALKALINE

ANNUALS

Annuals are plants that grow up, flower, and then die all within a single year — putting the gardener to the regular work of preparing their beds, planting them, and then clearing them away to make ready for fresh plantings. But if their lives are short, they can be gay indeed — few plants can make such a splash of colour as annuals. Unlike shrubs and perennials they don't call on you to make a long-term commitment: you can ring the changes as your fancy takes you — petunias one summer, marigolds the next... And in a new garden they are indispensable, giving you something to look at while your permanent plantings are still in their infancy.

Annuals are classed as **hardy** (planted in autumn to flower at the end of winter and through the spring), or as **half-hardy** and **tender** (these like warm weather and so are planted in spring for summer and autumn bloom). Pansies and sweet peas are hardy; zinnias and African marigolds

There's no need to plant annuals in boring, regimented rows. They look wonderful planted in mix-and-match groups, as here.

Removing the spent blooms from annuals (dead-heading them) keeps them tidy and prolongs flowering

tender. Some PERENNIAL plants have a habit of flowering themselves to death in their first year, so are usually regarded as annuals — petunias are the prime example.

Almost all annuals prefer sunshine, fertile soil, and regular watering. If you

take the trouble to remove spent flowers so that they don't have a chance to set seed, they will usually flower for longer. Try growing on a few annuals in 10 centimetre pots for planting out when they come into flower. Instant garden! It's an old head gardener's trick.

Aphids can destroy young shoots on plants and can also spread virus diseases.

APHIDS

Sap-sucking insects, aphids (or green-fly) have the ability to reproduce without the benefit of sex, so they can appear in enormous numbers, most familiarly on the soft young shoots of roses, but on many other plants too. They can be controlled by almost any insecticide (TOBACCO WATER is effective), but also by a thorough hosing to dislodge and drown them, or by the slightly messy method of squashing them between your fingers. Ladybirds relish them, and are to be welcomed.

It is important to get rid of aphids, because not only can they cripple young shoots, they also, by means not entirely understood, spread virus diseases.

ASH

The ash from burning wood, which includes prunings and weeds as well as the logs in your fuel stove, is a useful fertiliser, being rich in potassium — but you must store it under cover, for rain will wash the potassium out. It is somewhat ALKALINE, so don't put it on acid-loving plants like azaleas or camellias, though roses and strawberries appreciate it. The ash from coal and barbecue charcoal has little nutrient value, but you can put it on the soil anyway. Don't overdo it; coal ash is apt to be full of sulphur. Any ash can be helpful in improving the texture of a clay soil. Dig in a layer about 2 cm thick when you are preparing the beds, and thereafter dust it over them when the ash is available, lightly forking it in.

BACTERIAL DISEASES

Bacteria attack plants much less commonly than they do animals and people, which is fortunate, as bacterial plant diseases are very difficult to treat. Usually all you can do is burn infected plants to contain the outbreak. Examples are CLUBROOT in brassicas (the cabbage tribe) and bacterial scab on gladioli, usually treated by dipping the corms in deadly poisonous chloride of mercury, a substance you and I should avoid.

BAMBOO

Never mind that its beauty has been celebrated in the Orient for centuries, or that it is one of the best plants where you want height but not width — bamboo's underground runners can be frighteningly INVASIVE. You can try confining it to an almost-sunk tub, when it will need constant attention with the hose in summer (it is not at all drought-resistant), or you can keep an eye out for unwanted shoots late in spring — just break them off at ground level when they are still soft and brittle, touch the stub with GLYPHOSATE, and the plant won't try again until next year.

Old stems gradually die off and look tatty. To keep bamboo looking elegant, each year ruthlessly cut out all stems that are more than two years old in late summer after this year's new shoots have grown. Don't throw the stems away: trim off the side shoots for a supply of garden stakes.

Bamboo shoots are much used in Chinese cooking, but don't try to prepare your own unless you know exactly what you're doing: they are covered in minute, sharp bristles which can wreak havoc on your insides. Safer to buy them canned!

PLANTING A BARE-ROOT ROSEBUSH

Dig a hole large enough to spread the roots of the plant in, and deep enough for the bud union to be at soil level. Tip in a bucket of water, when it has drained off, top up with soil and mulch.

BARE-ROOT

During their winter dormancy, roses, many deciduous trees, fruiting and otherwise, and many herbaceous plants can cope with being lifted entirely from the soil, as long as their newly bare roots are not allowed to dry out. This makes them easy for nurseries to handle, and they are indeed usually sold

this way, often with the roots packed in peatmoss and wrapped in plastic. Don't accept any that look dried-out, with shrivelled stems or roots.

When you get them home, plant them as soon as possible, even if you only 'heel them in' in temporary quarters. Heeling in is simple — just make a soil trench, put the roots in, cover with soil and water. Planting is also straightforward.

BONSAI and such plants as container-grown camellias sometimes have their roots bared at repotting time. Tip the plant out of its pot, wash away as much of the old soil as possible with a strong jet from the hose, and *immediately* replant in the pot, carefully easing fresh soil in around the roots. A chopstick can be very useful for this. This takes a bit of trouble, but it can save having to buy a larger pot.

BEDDING

This is growing a mass of flowers in a flower bed, of course, but in English horticulture it has the specific meaning of planting the bed mainly with frost-tender flowers that have been started in a greenhouse, and 'bedded out' as they come into bloom for a summer display. Wealthy Victorian gardeners were known to show off by changing the bedding in the garden as often as in the bedrooms. Plants like geraniums, lobelias, petunias, even cannas, are traditional. Most of these 'bedding plants' don't need such cosseting in our mild climate, and we can plan our flower beds as year-round features.

BEES

Bee-keeping is a specialised branch of horticulture, and liable to have the neighbours up in arms if you decide to take it up. But bees are useful creatures to have in the garden — you are unlikely to have much fruit without them — and you should not spray with toxic chemicals when they are about. If a swarm takes up residence, call your local council, who will be able to put you in touch with a bee-keeper who will gladly take it off your hands.

Honey-eating birds occur in South Africa too, and our own honey-eaters will be attracted by such South African flowers as the cape honeysuckle (Tecomaria capensis).

BIENNIALS

A biennial is a plant with a two-year life cycle: it grows in its first year, then flowers, sets seed and dies in its second. The most familiar example is parsley, which usually dies down at the end of its first autumn, to come up again with flowers and seeds the following spring — much to the frustration of the gardener, who then has to plant more to keep up the supply of leaves for the kitchen (though the stalks and flowers are edible too). Foxgloves, canterbury bells, and wallflowers are biennials, though in our mild climate you can treat them as hardy ANNUALS: plant them early enough in the autumn and they will usually flower the following spring.

BIRDS

My mother adored persimmons and had a beautiful tree, as graceful as a Chinese painting. Never was it more beautiful than when the fruit began to ripen and the rosellas, all crimson and green and gold, descended on it for samples.

There are all sorts of ways to keep the birds from robbing your fruit — scarecrows; covering the trees with nets; hanging the branches like Christmas trees with strips of aluminium foil to dazzle and frighten; growing your fruit in a vast chicken-wire cage — but they aren't always effective, because the birds soon work out how to get round them. Try these methods by all means, but be prepared to have to pay tithes for the privilege of having birds around.

Encouraging birds to the garden is a much simpler matter. Just plant a variety of native plants, which will provide nectar, nesting places and shelter, and their own population of insects for insect-eating birds. You can plant fruit too; not the fruit you might want for your own table, but plants like cotoneasters and crabapples, even sunflowers, whose seeds parrots adore. Put a bell around the cat's neck if you have to, to warn the birds when it is about, and avoid the use of poisonous sprays as much as you can. Just make them welcome, and the birds will come.

Bird-attracting plants
Most native plants, including grevilleas, waratah, hakeas, banksias
New Zealand flax
Cotoneasters
Crabapples
Pyracantha

BLACK PLASTIC

Sheets of black plastic, usually masked with pebbles or pine chips, are much loved by some landscapers as a totally weed-proof and long-lasting mulch, but the stuff is best avoided. Not only does it suffocate the soil, it isn't as weed proof as all that: you have to leave gaps to insert your plants, and weeds can establish there too. Commercial strawberry growers use it to keep their fruit out of the mud, but in the garden, we should all prefer the traditional straw mulch (hence the name strawberry), which rots in due course, adding humus to the soil. Black plastic does find a use in lining the bed for a bog garden, and you can wrap celery plants (leaving the leaves sticking out at the top of the parcel) to BLANCH the stalks.

BLACK SPOT

One of the commonest diseases of the rose, and one of the most devastating, black spot kills any leaf it infects, seriously weakening the plant. It spreads readily from plant to plant, and there is no real cure. If you live in the sort of humid-summer climate (like Sydney's) where the fungus flourishes, a regular programme of spraying with fungicide (Triforine is well thought of) is needed, preferably starting before you see the first tell-tale fringed black spots on the lower leaves. Black spot spores can only attack a leaf that has been wet for about three hours, hence the common advice to water only the ground and not wet the rosebushes themselves. Red and pink varieties are usually more resistant to black spot than the yellows and flames. It is only prudent not to bother with varieties known to be susceptible to the disease; a good rose-grower will warn you of them.

A similar fungus sometimes attacks the fruit of apples and pears; control is the same.

BLANCHING

Whitening the shoots of asparagus and endives, and the stalks of celery to make them pale and tender is known as blanching. Traditionally this is done by

▲ *Some strains of sweet William will flower in their first year, but most are BIENNIALS, flowering in their second spring.*

▼ *Canterbury bells will bloom in their first spring if you plant them early in the autumn. They do best in cool climates.*

Bundling up celery in plastic to whiten the stalks and make the flavour sweeter.

heaping sand over the plant about three weeks before harvest, but celery can be bundled up in black plastic.

BLOOD AND BONE

Vegetarians will probably shun blood and bone, which is a by-product of the meat industry, but it is probably the most concentrated organic fertiliser, great for giving plants a quick boost, and just about the best 'activator' for the COMPOST heap there is. Sprinkle a handful or two on the heap after you have added a few centimetres of fresh material to it. Rich in nitrogen and phosphorus, it is very powerful stuff; spread the dark brown powder nearly as frugally as you would a chemical fertiliser, just sprinkling enough to colour the soil the way a cook sprinkles icing sugar on a cake. Its drawbacks are that it isn't cheap, and that its smell will probably have the dog digging frantically in the hope of finding the canine equivalent of King Solomon's Mines unless you water it in lavishly and at once.

BLUE

If you buy a plant described as 'blue' and find its flowers are a tone that your decorator would call 'lilac', don't go after the nursery for misrepresentation! The fact is that truly blue flowers are rather rare in nature, most blue flowers having at least an undertone of mauve. They are no less beautiful for that, and soft 'gardeners' blue' is a wonderful colour in the garden: it goes with everything, and can be used to blend stronger colours where white would be too sharp a contrast.

'Blue' foliage, such as that of the blue spruce and the various blue gums, is actually a steely grey, what the botanist would describe as *glaucous*.

'Blue' foliage plants

Many conifers, such as blue spruce (*Picea pungens* 'Glauca'), blue cedar (*Cedrus atlantica glauca*), some junipers, such as 'Grey Owl' and 'Meyeri', *Cupressus torulosa*
Eucalyptus cinerea
Eucalyptus crenulata
Eucalyptus globulosa (juvenile foliage)
Acacia baileyana (some forms)
Lavandula stoechas
Some succulents, such as *Kleinia*, *Sedum spathulifolium*

True blue flowers

Borage (*Borago officinalis*)
Alkanet (*Anchusa italica*)
Blue poppy (*Meconopsis baileyi*)
Blue butterfly bush
(*Clerodendrun ugandense*)
Baby blue-eyes (*Nemophila menziesii*)
Bearded iris (many newer cultivars)
Clitorea (*Clitorea ternata*)
Cornflower (*Centaurea cyanus*)
Chinese forget-me-not
(*Cynoglossum amabile*)
Chinese plumbago
(*Ceratostigma willmottianum*)
Forget-me-not (*Myosotis*)
Lechenaultia (*Lechenaultia biloba*)
Larkspurs and delphiniums
(*Delphinium* 'Pacific Giant' and
Delphinium 'Blue Butterfly')
Hydrangeas (in acid soil)
Salvias, perennial
(*Salvia patens uliginosa*)
Pride of Madeira (*Echium fashiosum*)
Lobelia (*Lobelia* 'Crystal Palace')
Morning glory (*Phartibis tricolor*
'Heavenly Blue')

King of the blue flowers, the delphinium comes in every shade from deep as ink to pale as a summer sky — and in purple, lilac and white too. All go beautifully together.

BOG GARDEN

An artificial bog can provide a congenial home for those plants that love wet feet, like the gorgeous Japanese irises, the swamp banksia (*Banksia robur*) or the gigantic-leaved *Gunnera manicata*. As well as the out-

Bog plants
Japanese and Louisiana irises
Daylilies
Hostas
Houttuyna cordata
Loosestrife (*Lythrum*)
Native broom (*Viminaria*)
Many ferns (check before you buy!)
Bergamot (*Monarda*)
Cannas
Perennial lobelias
Schizostylis coccinea

▲ *The soft pure blue of forget-me-nots, lovely in its own right and a perfect foil for taller spring flowers like daffodils or tulips. Once established, forget-me-knots will sow themselves forever.*

▼ *Bog plants often feature bold and luxuriant foliage as well as flowers, and look cool and refreshing no matter how hot and parched the rest of the garden may be. Here, among others, are skunk cabbage and rodgersias.*

and-out swamp lovers, such regular garden plants as daylilies, cannas and the perennial lobelias will flourish mightily too. And it's not difficult to make one. Choose a sunny site. The 'bog' will look most appropriate if it is low-lying, and you could associate it with a pond if you like. Don't make it too large, or you'll have to put on your Wellington boots to go weeding.

Dig out the soil from your chosen spot to a depth of half a metre or so, and line the hole with two thicknesses of black plastic sheeting. Punch some holes in the bottom with a garden fork, so that there will be some drainage to keep the soil from getting

▲ A successful bonsai should give the effect of a full-sized tree seen through the wrong end of a telescope.

▼ A mixed border of summer-blooming perennials, in harmonising tones of pink and mauve spiced wih yellow.

stagnant and sour, and fill up again with soil to which you have added as much organic matter as you can lay your hands on. Plant your plants. An edging of brick, stone or whatever suits your garden will both mask the edge of the plastic and keep the lawn from invading, which it will do with great delight.

You will need to water occasionally in warm weather to keep the ground wet, but the drainage holes should ensure that there won't be long-lasting puddles for mosquitoes to breed in; and the plants will benefit from an annual top dressing of organic fertiliser in the spring.

BONE MEAL

Sometimes called bone flour, this is blood and bone without the blood; it is the standard organic source of PHOSPHORUS. The phosphorus leaches from it only very slowly, so it is much less polluting than SUPERPHOSPHATE, and it is safe to use around delicate roots and seedlings — there need be little worry about burning them.

BONSAI

The art of dwarfing forest trees into miniature replicas of themselves originated in China a thousand years ago, but we in the West are most familiar with the way the Japanese practise it.

Confined as it is to a tiny pot, starved and pruned to within an inch of its life, a bonsai tree needs constant, devoted care: regular watering (daily or twice daily in the summer); pruning of both branches and roots; repotting; and occasional, carefully timed, minute doses of fertiliser. You can bring a bonsai tree inside to show it off, but only for a few days at a time: it must spend most of its life in a protected spot outdoors.

Training and shaping in any one of the several traditional styles calls for practice and an artist's eye, and whether you regard bonsai as one of the pinnacles of the gardener's art or as horticultural sadism, it is not for the casual gardener.

If you fancy the challenge, it is well worth joining your local bonsai society, where you can learn from the adept.

Some good border plants
Bearded irises
Iris sibirica and its cultivars
Hellebores
Daylilies
Pride of Madeira (*Echium*)
Gauera lindheimeri (white butterfly)
Stoker aster (*Stokesia*)
Most daisies
Dahlias
Agapanthus
Geraniums
Lavender, cistus and small, shrubby roses for the front
But the list is endless — just about any flowery plant that takes your fancy!
Coreopsis
Echinacea
Liatris
Hibiscus
Perennial phlox
Monarda
Shasta daisies
Rudbeckia
Lychnis

BORDERS

In Australia, we mean by a border a row or two of some low-growing plant to finish off the front of a flower bed or shrubbery. But we also admire the English **herbaceous border**, an artfully displayed collection of flowers, usually perennials, and by no means all low-growing. These are normally laid out in a long bed against a backdrop of a wall, hedge, or trees, to form a border to a lawn or path.

The English border is at its peak from June to October; in our mild climate we face the challenge of making

such a border interesting all year, and call on the aid of shrubs, roses, annuals, and bulbs as well as herbaceous plants, so making what the English would call a **mixed border.** Planning such a border brings out the artist in you as you arrange not only the colours of the flowers, but also their heights, shapes, and flowering times. Plant not in ones and twos, but in generous groups. Plants with good foliage, like irises, daylilies and hellebores, make a lasting contribution to the picture even when they aren't in bloom. If you use one or two of these lavishly, they can tie the whole scheme together so it isn't just a jumble.

BRASSICAS

Cabbages (green, red and ornamental), cauliflower, broccoli, Brussels sprouts and kohlrabi are all garden forms of *Brassica oleracea*; turnips and the various Chinese cabbages are close relatives, as are stocks and wallflowers. They are all subject to various soil-borne diseases, of which the crippling and incurable CLUB ROOT is the worst, which is why you mustn't grow any of them in the same place two years running or even follow one member of the tribe with another. See also CROP ROTATION.

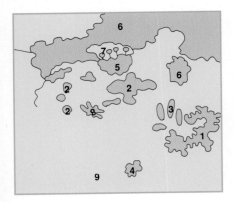

◀ 1. Rudbeckia 2. Ecinacea 3. Liatris 4. Hibiscus 'Southern Belle' 5. Perennial phlox 6. A green backdrop of shrubs 7. Shasta daisies 8. A daylily 9. Chrysanthemums, which will flower later.

Mizumi (Brassica oleracea japonica), a Japanese type of cabbage, with the characteristic four-petalled flowers of its tribe. Easy to grow, it is used in salads and stir-fries.

Watering & saving water

If you remember your high school science, photosynthesis is the process whereby plants take carbon dioxide from the atmosphere, and, aided by the energy of sunlight and the miraculous green substance CHLOROPHYLL, use it to build up their living substance, returning oxygen to the air for animals and humans to breathe. But they need hydrogen and oxygen too, and these they derive from water — a thirsty plant is a hungry one too. Which is why plants are sluggish in times of drought, and why watering is one of the gardener's main preoccupations.

At least in our dry country; visiting friends in England I was surprised to see they had no garden tap, something we take for granted. They were content to let their abundant rainfall take care of their garden's needs, for a tap and hose would have cost them more on the water rates — even there, water is a resource not to be squandered.

How much more so in Australia, the driest continent where gardens are made. A surprising proportion of the water we use goes on our gardens, simply wasted. Most local water supply authorities are forcing conservation on us all by progressively reducing the amount of water each household can use before excess rates become payable, so water wasted is money down the drain too.

THE GOLDEN RULE

Only water when your plants actually need it, and then water *thoroughly*. Any old country gardener, used to doling out the water from tanks and dams, will tell you it is better not to water at all, forcing your plants to send their roots deep into the subsoil, than to just wet the surface when it looks dry. This might give the plants a pick-me-up (and make you feel good) but it encourages them to keep their roots close to the surface to suffer when it dries out again.

Soils vary in the way they accept water: clay takes it in only slowly but dries out slowly too; sand takes it in very quickly but dries out fast and you need to water more often. Loam is the ideal, but all soils will be improved by adding as much organic matter as possible — yet another reason to have a compost heap. You might need to do a bit of experimenting to work out how much water you need for a thorough soaking. When the soil is dry, try putting the sprinkler on, or holding the hose, for ten minutes or so, and then, when any puddles have disappeared, digging down to see how far the water has gone (wet soil looks different from dry). If it's wet to, say, 10 centimetres, then you will know that you will probably need to water for half an hour to get the water down to 30 or 35 centimetres, which is where you want it.

CONTROLLING WIND IN THE GARDEN

Wind can dry out your garden as efficiently as it does the washing on the line, and shelter from the drying winds of summer is important.

1 The wind just jumps a solid wall or fence, creating turbulence on the other side.

2 A screen of foliage (or an open fence or trellis) breaks its force more effectively.

3 Wet foliage acts like an air-conditio[...] cooling the breeze that passes through it. [...] comfortable for both you and your plants!

4 A windbreak of trees or tall shrubs will give shelter for a distance of about eight times its height.

The water-thrifty garden need not be drab. Here, a collection of drought-tolerant plants from all over the world (gazanias from South Africa, lavender from France, bottlebrushes from Australia) make a blaze of colour all summer.

HOW OFTEN TO WATER?

You don't want to waste water by watering more often than you need, but then you do want to keep your plants happy. If they really get parched, they'll wilt, but if you watch carefully you'll learn to recognise the advance warnings. Leaves and flowers will look limp and lustreless; grass loses its springiness and retains your footprints. But it doesn't take long to develop the sixth sense that says 'That plant looks thirsty'. Don't be deceived by the surface soil looking dry; if you're in doubt, dig down a little to check.

Of course, you'll need to water more often when it's hot. But try, unless it's an emergency, not to water in the heat of the day, when much of your precious water will evaporate at once, either from the sprinkler or from wet leaves. Wetting the foliage of shade-loving plants like camellias when the sun is on them can be disastrous, as the water drops act like little lenses and the leaves get sunburned. Believe it or not, the best time to water is when it is actually raining; if you think a shower won't be adequate, you won't be as silly as you might feel if you supplement it with the hose.

As a general rule, it's better to get the water directly to the soil; but don't apply it faster than it can be absorbed, or you'll not only lose water from runoff, you will also run the risk of compacting the surface like a mud pie. On clay and silty soils this may mean that you can't turn the hose on full, so just be patient and keep it on for longer.

SPRINKLER SYSTEMS

Watering more lightly for a longer time is easier if you have enough taps to allow you to set two or three sprinklers at once, and shorter hoses are not only less of a bother, they also last longer. Do you have enough taps, or should you consider adding another one or two? Or even a fixed sprinkler system? These vary enormously in sophistication (and cost!) from simple do-it-yourself kits that just attach to the tap and provide either trickle nozzles (drippers) to deliver water slowly at the roots of plants where they are needed, or mini-sprinklers (mini-sprays), which will water an area of a couple of square metres each. These systems use small-size flexible black plastic tubing to distribute the water, and this can look pretty dreadful unless you can arrange to bury it, but you will then have to watch out when you dig. Make a plan to scale before you buy the kit, so that you can design an efficient layout, avoiding wasting water on pavements and paths. (The makers provide how-to-do-it instructions.) Buy extra sprinklers and drippers: they are so small that they are always clogging up and needing attention. Check them fairly often: you don't want to find out a nozzle isn't working by the death of some favourite plant. The drippers are just about the most water-thrifty things there are, but they are best for a permanent planting like a shrubbery, groundcover planting or a rose bed, because you need one for each plant, and in a vegetable or annual bed the tubes, like black spaghetti, get in the way of cultivating and replanting. You need fewer of the mini-sprays, so they are more flexible; but they need to sit about 35 centimetres above ground on long stalks, and can be awkward to hide. Most systems will allow you to use the two kinds interchangeably.

Going up the scale, you can get sprinklers that sit discreetly below ground and pop up when the water is turned on (the only kind for lawns), as well as timers that allow you to programme your watering weeks in advance, and even computer-controlled systems that sense when the soil is dry. These are best professionally designed and installed; the phone book should turn up a number of 'irrigation specialists' to talk to. Any fixed watering system is a great saver in time and trouble, and can save water too, provided that you can resist showing it off by turning it on all the time.

Sprinklers never distribute their water evenly: they almost always water more heavily towards the outside of their area than in the middle. You can gauge the pattern by putting out a row of old jam jars and seeing how much water is in each after running the sprinkler for a few minutes, but if you space fixed sprinklers so that each wets its neighbour, the irregularities will cancel out. Try to do the same with a sprinkler attached to the hose, by moving it to the edge of the area it watered before.

Sprinklers are best used in the evening, as hot sunshine can evaporate a lot of the spray before it even hits the ground. If you are like me and tend to wander off to find you've left the sprinkler on all night, a timer fitted to the tap is a good investment; they aren't expensive.

Quite a variety of sprinklers are available to fit on the end of the hose, but it isn't worth spending time on comparison shopping or building up a collection. The cheapest will do! Soaker hoses — long fat ones with many little holes — are valuable for those long narrow beds that seem to occur in every garden, but turn them upside down to avoid spraying water where you don't want it. Of course, you can just water with the hose in your hand, but that gets boring and it's very easy to give up before the job is finished.

It isn't true that all Australian plants are drought-resistant, but many are, and with little more assistance than rainfall they can give a show like this.

Lawns are the biggest consumers of water, and in dry inland areas it is worth considering eliminating grass altogether, flooring the garden with paving. Here red scoria has been used effectively — but might look less like a carpark with some trees to soften and shade it.

MULCHES are great water savers, keeping the soil cool and blocking evaporation from the surface, but their greatest benefit is in keeping weeds down. For the most important single thing you do to save water is to keep the garden weeded. Far more moisture is lost from the soil by transpiration from plants than by evaporation from the soil itself, and weeds are very efficient at this — it's one of the ways they are able to flourish so mightily that they become weeds! It makes no sense at all to allow plants you don't even want to rob water from those you do.

THE WATER-THRIFTY LAWN

It has been estimated that lawns take nearly 80 per cent of garden water, and that half of that is usually wasted. Here even more than elsewhere, the golden rule of watering thoroughly but not often applies. It's very easy to get the lawn, which is not very deep rooted to begin with, addicted to the sprinkler. Even in the hottest weather, a well-managed lawn shouldn't need watering more than once a week, but the time to start training it is in spring, before the hot weather starts. Don't worry if you can't water it at all during drought. Leave it to get a bit long (close mowing reduces the grass's reserves of strength) and it will recover well enough when the rain comes. After all, grass in nature isn't springtime green all year. Naturally, you will have chosen your grass species for their ability to stand up to your local conditions.

Is your lawn simply too big? Would it be an improvement to the design of the garden to replace part of it with less thirsty groundcovers or shrubs, or even with paving or gravel? Paving needn't be laid on concrete: if you lay bricks or the like on a bed of sand, water will percolate down through the joints to the soil beneath where the roots of trees can find it.

CHOOSE YOUR PLANTS WITH CARE

You can save a lot of water if you make plants that will flourish on your local rainfall the backbone of your plantings. A tour of the neighbourhood during the next dry spell will give you plenty of ideas, and no doubt your local nursery will have more. Natives are a standby, being bred to the climate, but there are many plants from other countries with climates similar to our own to choose from. And favourites that need pampering can always be grouped together in choice spots — say around the patio or near the front door — where they can be best enjoyed.

The plants will thank you if these choice spots are out of the wind, which can dry the garden as efficiently as it does the washing on the line. It isn't always possible in the suburbs to plant windbreak trees, but shrubs and fences can still do the job. Don't have fences too solid, or the wind will simply ricochet off them all over the garden; open foliage or a trellis-type structure will filter the breeze. Frost can dry the garden out too, and you may have to water in a dry winter to compensate.

CHECK THOSE TAPS!

And, before you do anything, check your taps and connections for leaks; a dripping tap can waste thousands of litres of water before you notice it.

We usually think of bromeliads as indoor plants, but these assorted aechmeas are perfectly happy outdoors in a shady, frost-free spot. The exotic flowers are very long-lasting.

BROMELIADS

A family of plants, the Bromeliaceae, mostly from South America, of which the pineapple is the most familiar example. Many are **epiphytes**, which conserve water by arranging their stiff leaves in a hollow rosette, from the centre of which an often stunning spray of flowers arises. Bromeliads include such plants as aechmeas, billbergias and vriesias, which are desirable indoor plants, and can be grown outside (they like shade) in warm, humid climates. They don't have much in the way of roots, so only need a pot large enough not to fall over under the weight of the plant. Watering is simple; just keep the 'vase' in the centre of each rosette full (you can add dilute MANURE WATER or liquid fertiliser occasionally), and sufficient water will trickle to the roots.

BUDDING

The simplest and easiest form of grafting, budding was described by one of Shakespeare's characters as 'improving a base character by inserting beneath its bark a bud of nobler race'. Budding was known and practised by the Romans, who used it for roses and fruit trees, just as we do today. Tradition calls for the use of a budding or grafting knife, but a fresh razor blade can serve just as well. Roses and citrus are usually budded in late spring, other fruit trees in autumn.

BUDS

A bud is, of course, an unopened flower, but it is also the little bump on a stem, in the axil (the 'armpit') of a leaf, from which a shoot will grow. Recognising such buds (or *eyes*) and what sort of shoot, flowering or leafy, will grow from them is half the art of pruning.

Growth buds on a dormant branch

BUDDING IS THE EASIEST FORM OF GRAFTING

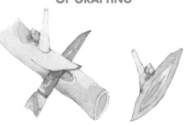

1 *With a sharp knife, cut the bud from the stem with a sliver of bark, leaving a bit of leaf stalk attached to serve as a handle. Don't let it dry out — hold it in your lips if need be.*

2 *Make a shallow T-shaped incision in the bark of the understock (previously grown from a cutting or seed) and gently lift the resulting flaps of bark. If it won't lift easily, water the plant heavily and try again in a day or two.*

3 *Slip the bud in behind the flaps, trimming off the top if it won't all fit.*

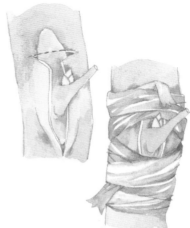

4 *Bind all together firmly with raffia or budding tape. If the bud takes, the leaf-stalk will drop off in a week or so. The raffia or tape will rot in due course. In winter, the stock is cut off just above the bud, which will grow away in spring.*

BULBS

Look at an onion and you have seen what a bulb is: a complete plant, leaves, next year's flower and all, reduced by Nature to a compact package. It's a marketing man's idea of the perfect plant, one that can be put in a box (or a bag), packaged attractively, and displayed on a shop shelf without the shop assistant having to worry about giving it light and water.

Unfortunately, shop people are inclined to forget that bulbs are alive and not immortal; it's not at all uncommon to see the pretty packets sitting, full priced, on supermarket shelves long after the end of the planting season with the poor, shrivelled bulbs at their last gasp, if not already dead. And even in the proper season (autumn for spring-flowering bulbs, such as TULIPS, daffodils, freesias; late winter or spring for summer flowerers, such as gladioli and hippeastrums), they can be bruised by

The season of spring bulbs is glorious but brief, and it is a good idea to plant bulbs among perennials or low shrubs, which will hide their declining foliage and provide follow-on flowers. These are hyacinths and tulips, both happiest in a cool-winter climate.

BULB PLANTING CHART

Bulb	When to Plant	Planting depth	Set apart	Height	Colours	Flowering
Anemone	Feb–Apr	10 cm	10–12 cm	15–20 cm	Red, blue, pink, white	Aug–Sept
Hyacinth	Feb–Apr	15 cm	15 cm	25–30 cm	Blue, white, pink, cream	Sept
Freesia	Feb–Apr	10 cm	10 cm	20 cm	All colours	Sept
Grape Hyacinth (Muscari)	Feb–Apr	10 cm	10 cm	10 cm	Blue	Aug–Sept
Iris, Dutch	Feb–Apr	15 cm	15 cm	35–40 cm	Blue, white, yellow	Sept–Oct
Tulip	Feb–Apr	15 cm	15cm	40 cm	All colours except blue	Sept–Oct
Bluebell (Spanish)	Feb–Apr	10 cm	10 cm	20 cm	Blue, pink	September
Triteleia (Ipheion uniflorum)	Feb–Apr	8–10 cm	8–10 cm	8 cm	Pale blue	Aug–Oct
Ranunculus	Feb–Apr	8 cm	10 cm	20 cm	All colours except blue	September
Daffodil						Aug–Sept
Jonquil	Feb–Apr	15 cm	10–15 cm	35 cm	Yellow, white, white and pink	July
(Narcissus tazetta)						July
Snowflake (Leucojum)						July
Madonna lily	April	Just below surface	15 cm	50 cm	White	Nov
All other lilies	May–Aug	15 cm	15–20 cm	50–150 cm	All except blue	Dec–Apr
Nerine	Dec	At surface	10 cm	30 cm	Red, pink, white	Feb–Mar
Crinum	Aug–Oct	At surface	35 cm	50 cm	Pink, white	Summer
Hippeastrum	July–Aug	Just below surface –5 cm	15 cm	30–40 cm	Red, pink, white	Nov–Dec
Gladiolus	Aug–Dec	10 cm	15 cm	30–50 cm	All colours	Nov–Apr

rough handling. So when you buy, make sure the bulb is still in good heart, firm and plump; reject any that are at all soft or spongy, shrivelled, or mouldy. LILIES (LILIUM) are a special case: lacking the protective skin or tunic of most bulbs, they can't stay out of the ground for long, and should be chosen with particular care. Reject any that don't still have substantial roots attached. As a general rule, the larger bulbs are the best buy, but don't forget that the size of the bulb varies enormously with the species.

Plan on planting as soon as possible after you get the bulbs home; there's no advantage in letting them sit around out of the ground. (But TULIPS can be chilled in the refrigerator before planting.)

Planting is simplicity itself: make a hole in the chosen spot, pop in the bulb, and cover it up again. The rule of thumb is to set the nose of the bulb as deep as the bulb is tall, but that isn't critical: most bulbs have the ability to adjust the depth to suit themselves. You can, if you like, bury a handful of old manure or a teaspoon or so of artificial fertiliser at the bottom of the hole, covering it over so the bulb doesn't touch it; but most bulbs flower on the strength already stored in the bulb, and as long as the soil is halfway decent and they get their share of water they should do well.

It is *after* flowering that you need to start pampering with fertiliser, for this is when the bulb is building itself up for next year. The foliage may be getting tatty, but don't try to encourage it to die down quickly, and do resist the temptation to cut it down until it has quite died off. It is, however, a good idea to remove the spent flowers so that the plant will put its strength into the bulb rather than into making seeds.

Most bulbous plants multiply into clumps by making baby bulbs (offsets); with time the clumps may get overcrowded and then you will need to lift and divide them. This is easiest at the end of the dying down period, when there is still some foliage to remind you where the bulbs are. If you need to cultivate a bed where bulbs are hiding, a fork is safer than a spade;

nothing makes one feel sillier than unearthing a bulb cut in half.

See also CORMS and TUBERS.

BUSHFIRES

Natural to the ecology of the bush, but horrible if they strike your home, bushfires are a hazard if you live near bushland or even grazing land, which can also burn ferociously. Keeping a clear firebreak between your property and the bush reduces the hazard, but you should think very carefully before making a bushland-type garden. Nature may not understand that you don't want your native shrubs, most of which

are highly flammable, and their leafy mulch burnt. Keeping the garden (and the roof gutters) free of leafy debris is prudent too. Consider installing a sprinkler system, even if you don't water the garden that often: many a house has been saved by turning on the sprinklers when the family has been forced to flee. Empty dams and water tanks are a small price to pay.

Clad in trellis instead of the traditional, bug-harbouring tea-tree branches, this bush house looks as smart as paint. The roof could be covered in shade cloth or lightly-foliaged creepers such as moonflowers to give extra summer shade.

BUSH HOUSES

The old-fashioned bush house, covered with tea-tree branches, is rarely seen these days, but they provided a useful spot to grow delicate plants like orchids and ferns that needed shade and shelter from hot and cold winds. The Americans build *lath houses*, the shade being given by closely spaced timber laths or battens, both as shelters for plants and to make places for sitting out. This is a nice idea; such a structure could well form a pleasant extension to the house. You could cover it with shade cloth also. I once saw an unused clothes hoist tented with shade cloth to make an improvised bush house; it didn't give much room for people, but it housed some stunning orchids.

BUTTERFLIES

Biologists distinguish butterflies from moths by the shape of their antennae, but most of us do so by colour — butterflies wear bright tones, moths dowdier beige and grey. Both spend their youth as CATERPILLARS, which are apt to be a nuisance, though butterfly caterpillars rarely come in devastating numbers. (The study of butterflies and moths is called lepidoptery; if you don't know the name of a particular butterfly or its caterpillar, you can plead never having studied it.) Encouraging butterflies is simply a matter of planting plants they and their caterpillars

Plants to attract butterflies
Almost all daisies
Citrus
Sedum spectabile
Butterfly bush (*Buddleia*)
Blue butterfly bush
(*Clerodendrum ugandense*)
Bougainvillea
Petunias
Grapes
Tea-trees (*Leptospermum*)
Bottlebrush (*Callistemon*)

frequent — butterflies mostly fly in summer, and almost all summer flowers will attract them. Many weeds, such as dock and nettles, provide food for caterpillars and there will be more butterflies if the garden is a little less than immaculate. And be restrained in your use of poison sprays.

BUYING PLANTS

After making sure that your chosen plant is in fact the variety you want (read the label!), check that the plant is alive and kicking. This isn't as silly as it sounds: accidents (as Oscar Wilde has said) occur in the best-regulated families, and supermarkets are notorious for keeping plants in stock until even the most uninformed salesperson can see that they are dead. If the plant has leaves, they should be green and fresh; reject out of hand any plant that is wilting or showing signs of disease. If it hasn't got leaves, and isn't expected to at that time of year, are the stems plump and firm, or shrivelled and withered looking? Watch BARE-ROOTED stock (roses, deciduous trees, lilies, the crowns of perennials, and the like) very carefully here. If they have dried out, they are likely to be done for. On the other hand, if they are kept too moist and warm, they are apt to weaken themselves by shooting prematurely.

Beware of plants that are pot-bound. Not only are they likely to be starving, once planted their roots may well continue to go round and round forever, never taking possession of their new home. Tell-tale signs are a plant that looks too big for its pot (and which may be offered at a bargain price to get rid of it); roots growing out of the drainage holes at the bottom, or showing at soil level; and a general air of malaise — which should lead you to reject any plant. If a plant doesn't look flourishing, don't buy it! It goes without saying that no reputable nursery allows weeds to compete with its plants.

Plants that can be made to look impressive in their nursery pots, preferably covering themselves with flowers — like fuchsias and rhododendrons — practically sell

A gorgeous butterfly, feasting on a spray of lilac. Flat-faced flowers like this are most butterflies' favourites.

themselves, and nurseries love them for that reason. Others, equally desirable, never look much in their youth — the rare and lovely climbing hydrangea for instance — and you need to be aware of this.

Many varieties will be available in a range of sizes. By all means pay the extra for larger, older, plants if you are in a hurry, but remember that a younger plant will often establish more easily and catch up to the 'advanced' one surprisingly quickly.

BUYING PLANTS BY MAIL

It often surprises people to hear that you bought a choice plant through the mail, but glance through any gardening magazine and you'll find nurseries offering an astonishing range of plants by post, often rarities that the local garden centre hasn't even heard of. Often the plants will be cheaper too. You lose the advantage of examining the plants before you buy, but a nurseryman who takes advantage of this to send inferior stock won't stay in business for long. And it's up to you to

be sure the plant will grow in your area!

The advertisement, or the CATALOGUE that will usually be sent on request, will detail how the order is to be paid for (most like a cheque or credit card authorisation with the order) and what the carriage charges will be. Always note on your order whether a similar variety can be substituted if your first choice is already sold out; it saves confusion. Often you won't want a substitute but a refund, but on the other hand you might get a pleasant surprise or two. Most likely, you'll be ordering ahead of the planting season; it's reasonable to expect an acknowledgement of the order, with advice when it will be dispatched.

Obviously, it's easiest to post plants that don't have to be accompanied by soil, like seeds, bulbs, or roses, but nurseries specialising in mail order are expert at packing and sending shrubs, seedlings, and even trees so that they arrive in good order. (Bulky and heavy packages are often sent by rail.) When the parcel arrives, open it at once (plants need air to breathe) and check that everything is as you wanted it. Don't delay writing to the nursery if it isn't, or if the plants have been damaged in the post. And then don't delay planting!

If you're planning to buy from overseas, check first with the Department of Agriculture how the quarantine regulations will affect you, and don't forget that the seasons in the Northern Hemisphere are the opposite of ours, so that plants from there are unlikely to arrive at our normal planting time.

CARNIVOROUS PLANTS

Plants that catch insects to supplement their diet — like sarracenias, sundews and the legendary Venus fly-trap — are fascinating, but they aren't very easy to grow. Most like a damp spot and shade; but they are all very sensitive to pollution, and the fluoride and other things found in tap water will kill them quickly. Water them with rainwater, or, better yet, buy distilled water for them. Don't expect them to live long — they don't like cultivation. While the carnivorous plants derive much nourishment from their prey in the wild, they do appreciate some fertiliser in the garden. Manure water is best — artificial fertilisers are apt to be too salty. It's fun to tickle the leaves of a Venus fly-trap to make them snap shut, but don't do it often, or the plant will get exhausted. Truly!

CARPET BEDDING

Fashionable in Queen Victoria's day, carpet bedding is rarely seen now except occasionally in public gardens. A bed (or beds) is cut out of a lawn, and planted with ground-hugging flowers and coloured-leaved plants arranged in elaborate patterns, to make a flat carpet of colour. You can't walk on it, of course, though sometimes the result is such that one wishes someone would.

CATALOGUES

You really know you've been bitten by the gardening bug when you start reading nursery catalogues in bed — they are the stuff of horticultural fantasy! Of course, whether they be mere duplicated price lists or lavish productions filled with coloured pictures of plants grown to the highest perfection, they are intended to tempt you to buy. Nurserymen are lovers of plants (they have to be; there are easier ways to make a living these days), and tend to write *con amore*, so that a flower won't be just 'yellow' but 'golden', not plain red but 'vivid scarlet'; while if it is normally 2 centimetres across, one of 3 centimetres will be 'very large'; if the plant is tricky to grow it 'rewards every care'; if it is a little different from its predecessors it is hailed as a 'completely new break' in plant breeding...and so on. This isn't really the language of slick salesmanship; it is a kind of gardener's jargon of such antiquity that it is rarely questioned. You still need to take it all with the proverbial grain of salt, but nurserymen are often astonishingly frank about the limitations and faults of what they have to sell.

Don't forget that the prices quoted don't remain forever. Make sure you have a current catalogue before you send your cheque.

See also BUYING PLANTS BY MAIL.

Carpet bedding at its best (or worst, depending on your point of view!) in a park in Dublin. Here the pattern is made from different-coloured succulents, but you could use low-growing annual flowers such as bedding begonias, lobelias, sweet alice, and dwarf French marigolds, maybe with a clump of cannas as a taller centrepiece.

A plague of caterpillars, munching a crinum leaf to shreds. If you don't want to use chemicals, spray with Dipel, which contains a bacterium (Bacillus thuringiensis) that will kill them off.

CATERPILLARS

Whether they grow up to be butterflies or moths, caterpillars eat leaves and are thus a nuisance in the garden. Birds usually keep them sufficiently under control, and you can squash the odd one or two by hand, but if you have a major invasion of cabbage moth caterpillars or the various types that cluster on the shoots of native plants, a spray with derris (rotenone) will kill them off.

Avoid contact with processional caterpillars, the hairy ones that walk Indian-file along twigs, especially on eucalypts. The hairs can break off in your skin, causing inflammation and misery.

CHEMICALS: USING THEM WISELY

There is a place for artificial fertilisers, for insecticides, fungicides and weedkillers in modern gardening. No matter how ardently you embrace the principles of ORGANIC gardening, there are some situations where a chemical is useful. It's difficult to fertilise a lawn with COMPOST or MANURE: an artificial: lawn fertiliser does the job better. A pot plant, with only a small amount of soil to find nourishment in, needs the concentrated nutrients of slow-release fertiliser, though it will still appreciate a top-dressing of rich compost. Sometimes one is faced with a plague

that just has to be sprayed, or persistent weeds that will only go away after a dose of GLYPHOSATE.

Learn to listen to your plants, to understand what they need, before you rush for the quick fix. If a plant is looking sad, does it really need to be sprayed or given a dose of chemical fertiliser? Might it just be suffering from drought? (water it), too much sunshine or shade? (transplant it, or thin the branches of the tree that's shading it), or from the soil around it being compacted by walking on its bed? (cultivate).

Could you pull that weed out in less time than it takes to find where you've put the weedkiller, or squash that caterpillar with less effort than is needed to get out the spray gun, mix up the poison, spray it on, and clean up the equipment afterwards? That bug may be the advance scout of an invading army, but then it may not; wait and see. If the army arrives, then is the time for the spray gun.

You can trust the makers of chemicals not to under-prescribe; don't fall into the habit of thinking that if a little does good, then twice as much will be twice as good. It won't; at best the extra chemical will be wasted, at worst it might do harm. Sprays applied too strongly may scorch the leaves they are meant to protect and harm desirable insects; too much fertiliser can burn foliage too (be especially careful in fertilising lawns), and is likely to upset the micro-organisms in the soil. Try two applications of half the amount of fertiliser, spaced a couple of weeks apart, rather than one big one; spot treat the weed rather than blanket spray the entire area. See if a less toxic spray will kill the bug. Home-made insecticides like TOBACCO WATER are often as effective as the powerful insecticides. And, as not many people use them, there is less risk of the insects developing resistance to them.

Think of garden chemicals as playing the same sort of role in the garden as drugs and vitamins do in ordinary life; you wouldn't try to live on a diet of pills or rush onto a course of antibiotics if you were just feeling a little poorly. So it is with the garden.

CHLOROPHYLL

This is the pigment that makes leaves green and plays a vital role in photosynthesis, the still rather mysterious process by which plants draw upon the energy of sunlight to make their food and substance from water and the carbon dioxide in the air. If a plant is getting insufficient sunlight, it will try to compensate by making more chlorophyll than normal, and its leaves will be an unnaturally dark green; conversely, too much sun may make them pale and yellowish. An alert gardener will notice this and move the plant to a more suitable position.

See also VARIEGATED LEAVES.

Lacking leaves, cacti rely on the chlorophyll in their stems; but the red star cactus (Gymnocalycium mihanovichii) has none, and must be grafted onto a green cactus to survive.

CHLOROSIS

In medicine, a greenish look about a patient's complexion: in gardening, just the opposite, an equally unhealthy *lack* of green in a plant. It can be caused by a shortage of NITROGEN, more rarely by an unavailability of iron in an excessively ALKALINE soil, or by too much light (see CHLOROPHYLL), or by the total exclusion of light, as when you leave the picnic blanket on the lawn and come back several days later to find the grass beneath it has turned yellow.

Gardening in containers

A plant in a container is a prisoner, entirely dependent on its gardener for its welfare. In the open ground, it can send its roots as wide and deep as it is able in search of water and food, and so can the other living things that share the soil with it. In a pot they can't, so you have to do it for them.

So why grow plants in containers at all? Nurseries do it because it's easier for their customers to take home a potted plant and plant it out with the minimum of disturbance than to dig one out of the ground. And you can 'grow on' the baby plants you propagate yourself until they are ready for their permanent homes. Growing new plants in pots means you have to give the plants constant attention, which works to their advantage, because you can give them the best of everything. This is a reason for growing an adult plant in a container too, of course, so you can give it just the soil it likes, water it just when it needs it, and move it in and out of the sun as needed. And if you don't actually have any soil to make a bed in, on a patio or verandah or indoors, then containers are the answer.

WHAT KIND OF CONTAINER?

If the container is only a temporary home, then the best kind to choose is the sort of back plastic pot that nurseries use, sized so that it is just a little larger than the plant's root

A really fancy container like this Victorian cast iron vase with its ornate handles can upstage any plant grown in it, and it is best to keep the planting simple.

The big Italian pots with their moulded decorations of garlands and lion masks were originally intended for lemon trees, but almost any shrub will look wonderful in them. It isn't really a good idea to stand an outdoor pot in a saucer, as it will fill up with water during rain, and the plant may drown.

ball. If there's more soil than the roots can occupy fairly quickly, the soil is likely to get sour from all the watering. The rule of thumb is a pot about half as wide again as the root ball. Infant plants go into the smallest pots; transfer them as they outgrow the pot into ones a size or two larger, the speed of the progression depending on how fast they grow. Try to keep the pots themselves shaded by standing them close together; black plastic can get hot in summer sun. You can reuse a pot that held a plant from the nursery, but wash it out and wipe the inside with bleach first, in case any trace of soil-borne diseases remains.

A permanent display pot, however, needs to set the plant off, something black plastic does rather poorly. You have a great choice of materials.

◆ **Fancy plastic** has the disadvantage that it can *look* cheap, though some of the newer kinds give a convincing simulation of other materials, like terracotta. Plastic can also be so light that a big plant will be always blowing over in the breeze, and it doesn't always last all that long, as sunlight can make it brittle. Fancy colours like pink and blue are apt to upstage their plants — subdued tones of green or brown are much nicer.

◆ **Wood** — old wine barrels, specially made planter boxes or the more elaborate VERSAILLES TUB — looks handsome, is light enough to handle, is cool for the roots and, if you choose western red cedar, teak, or treated pine, lasts for years. Wood is the material of choice for window boxes.

◆ **Concrete** (like timber) is only used for large-sized containers, and is awfully heavy. Some manufacturers tint concrete to look like sandstone, which can look pleasant, or you can mellow it by washing it down with MANURE WATER to encourage moss.

One of the joys of growing flowers in containers is that you can bring them centre-stage when they are at their best, and retire them to a discreet corner for their off seasons. Notice how the choice of a single material (terracotta) gives harmony to a collection of containers of different sizes and shapes.

A fancy container needn't imply a fancy plant. Here nasturtiums are given importance by being displayed in a stone urn.

◆ **Terracotta** comes in all sizes from tiny to enormous, some of the larger Italian designs being extremely elegant. Its warm colour is also flattering to any plant you might put in it. Its porosity means that it dries out faster than plastic, which can be an advantage in helping prevent over-watering, but a disadvantage in that fertiliser salts tend to seep through and leave a white 'bloom' on the outside, though this does wash off.

◆ **Glazed and decorated pottery** is expensive and very fragile, but it can look very nice, especially indoors. BONSAI pots are usually glazed in muted colours. Check that there are adequate drainage holes, as some of the handsomest Chinese pots are intended for goldfish rather than plants.

The size of a display pot is a matter of proportion: you want adequate space for the plant's roots, but you don't want the whole thing looking bottom-heavy. The design can contribute to the mood of your garden — half-barrels for an informal, rustic effect, more elaborate containers like Italian lemon tubs for a formal garden.

PLANTING

Having chosen your plant and the container, there are still a couple of preliminary things to do. First, prepare the container. Wood might need a coat of teak oil or varnish inside, for preservation (not creosote, which is not only messy but also harmful to the roots); new concrete should be washed out in case of excess alkalinity; terracotta should be soaked in water, or it will absorb most of the first couple of waterings. Tradition then calls for a few pieces of broken pot over the drainage holes to keep the soil from either blocking them or falling out, but with plastic pots this isn't really needed, and a piece of bronze or plastic flywire over large holes does the job just as well. It keeps worms from getting in too; however useful they may be in the open ground, they rapidly wear out their welcome in the confines of a pot. A couple of centimetres of gravel in the bottom will help drainage, which is all-important, since the limited amount of soil in a container goes sour very quickly if it gets waterlogged.

Don't load up with soil from the garden because the plant will rapidly exhaust its humus, and constant watering compacts it like cement. Make up an enriched and porous mix equal parts of coarse sand, the finer compost from the compost heap, and your best soil from the garden, boosted with a little slow-release fertiliser like Osmocote, or buy a ready-made potting mix.

Then you can plant your plant, filling in around it gently — a chopstick is useful for making sure you get the soil in without air spaces — and setting the final soil level about 2 centimetres or so below the rim to allow space for watering.

LOOKING AFTER CONTAINER PLANTS

Watering is indeed the main attention that a pot plant needs; it won't do the plant any good if you keep letting it dry out to wilting point. And if it does get that dry, the soil ball will shrink, and the next watering will just run out through the gap between it and the pot. If this does happen, it's best to sit the pot in a container of water for a couple of hours, so that the water can be absorbed from below. Frequent watering will leach nutrients from the soil rather quickly, and pot plants need regular fertilising. This is one of the few instances where artificial fertilisers really are indispensable, and the best are the slow-release pelleted kinds, which last for several weeks; the fairly small amount you need offsets their high price.

REPOTTING

Eventually the plant will exhaust its soil, and repotting into a larger pot will be called for. If you want to keep the same one, then you may need to use ROOT PRUNING or BARE-ROOTING to make room for fresh soil. Happily, this isn't a frequent chore: yearly is often enough.

CHOOSING PLANTS FOR A PURPOSE

Nothing is more frustrating to a nurseryman than to be asked to recommend a plant that might, you know, look nice in the front garden. In choosing a plant, ask yourself what purpose it is to serve in the garden. Shade? Privacy? A windbreak? A groundcover? Or just a splash of colour next to the front steps? There's no reason why it shouldn't serve more than one: a fruit tree might equally screen an undesirable view, or a groundcover give flowers. Then you can form a mental picture of the sort of plant that you'll need — a spreading tree for shade, a tall shrub for privacy, annuals or roses for cutting — and the choice will be much easier.

CLIMBING PLANTS

It is said that if a climbing plant twines clockwise in the Northern Hemisphere, it will grow anti-clockwise in the Southern. Maybe so, but not all climbers twine their shoots around their supports the way wisteria and morning glory do. Some, like passionfruit and grapes, grasp their support with tendrils, and yet others cling by small roots all along their stems, like ivy and Virginia creeper. These last will attach themselves to a wall or fence without the need for a trellis (they will get the idea more quickly if you don't let the young plants get too dry at the root), but for the others you will need to provide one, either of wood or wire. Climbing roses and bougainvillea need to be tied to their trellis with string; their habit is simply to wave their arms about in the hope of leaning on something, and trained to a wall they are really a kind of ESPALIER.

It is a good idea to train any wall-covering climber horizontally at first, to counter its natural tendency to rush up to the sunshine and leave the lower part bare.

CLIMBING PLANTS

1 *Left to themselves, most vines tend to rush up to the top of their wall or trellis, resulting in a bunch of growth above and bare legs below. To counteract this, train the shoots of a young vine horizontally at first.*

2 *Shoots will arise all along the horizontal branches, and you will get much more even, top-to-bottom coverage.*

CLIPPING

Clipping a hedge is a tedious job — not difficult in itself (as long as your shears are sharp), but needing concentration if the result is to be even. A light stake, marked with the height and width — coloured electrician's tape is useful — and used to check as you go makes life a lot easier. Fancy TOPIARY is best clipped freehand, and you'll probably want a smaller than usual pair of shears. If you use an electric hedge trimmer, you'll need to use it while the growth is still young and soft enough for it, and of course, you won't cut the flex and shock yourself. Large leaves, like those of camellias or photinias, will call for more careful trimming with secateurs if you object to seeing them cut in half by regular shearing.

CLONES AND CLONING

A clone is a living thing reproduced from a single individual without the benefit of sex. All clones are exactly alike. Cloning animals, let alone people, is the stuff of science fiction, but it is

done with plants all the time: every time you take cuttings or divide a clump of perennials (see DIVISION) you are making a clone. Most CULTIVARS, like the rose 'Queen Elizabeth' or the grevillea 'Ned Kelly', are clones, which is why we don't propagate them sexually, that is by seed: we want our new plants guaranteed identical to the original.

CLUB ROOT

A bacterial disease that affects the roots of BRASSICAS, that is cabbages and their close relatives, which include cauliflowers, broccoli, Brussels sprouts, kohlrahbi and the various Chinese cabbages, as well as stocks and wallflowers. The roots become swollen

Bougainvillea neither has tendrils, nor does it twine: it makes long shoots that hoist themselves up into any convenient tree. It needs to be trained, pruned, and tied in place if it is grown against a fence. Here the crimson 'Mrs Butt' crowns a very ordinary fence with colour, and its thorns will deter even the most evil-minded intruder. But keep it under control, for the safety of innocent passers-by!

and unable to function properly, and the plants, if not killed, are severely stunted.

As it is almost impossible to rid the soil of the bacteria by chemicals, you should practise CROP ROTATION, not growing any of the tribe in the same place two years running, to ensure epidemics of the bacteria cannot build up — or if they are present, that they starve to death while the soil is cabbage-free. Other non-susceptible plants (just about anything) can occupy the ground between brassica crops.

COMPACTED SOIL

The weight of the heavy equipment that builders need can crush the structure of soil (especially clay) so that it sets like cement, to the dismay of any plants trying to force their roots through it. The first task of the owner of a new house and garden should be to mend the damage by thorough CULTIVATION either by DOUBLE DIGGING or the easier but less effective method of hiring a rotary hoe. The soil under a lawn can compact over the years under the impact of feet, let alone

cars allowed to park on it, and here the remedy is an annual aeration with a special spiked gadget, called a lawn aerator, which you can hire. One of the (few) benefits of having a sandy soil is that it will compact less readily than heavier ones; if your soil is clayey or silty, think twice before you allow parking on the front lawn.

COMPANION PLANTS

The belief that certain plants exert a beneficial effect on their neighbours while others do the opposite is as old as gardening. In some instances there is scientific evidence in support: it seems that the roots of marigolds (French and African, not calendulas) secrete substances that frighten away NEMATODES (eelworms), a fairly common pest of tomatoes, and so help the tomatoes to flourish; and that the common reluctance of lawn to grow beneath eucalypts is at least partly due to the secretions of certain insects that live on the eucalypts' leaves. But often the ancient wisdom is based on notions of the compatibility or otherwise of the plants' horoscopes — which you can

believe or not as you choose! It is often said that planting garlic among rosebushes will keep aphids away from them, whiffs of garlic when you stoop to smell the roses being a small price to pay. Perhaps so; I tried it once, admittedly using garlic chives rather than garlic itself, but the aphids just ate the garlic chives, and then migrated to the roses. The lists below give suitable and unsuitable companion plantings — but lists and combinations suggested vary greatly, according to which book you are reading.

Happy marriages
Roses and garlic
Corn and beans
Tomatoes and marigolds
Onions and carrots
Potatoes and beans
Potatoes and cabbage
Tomatoes and onions
Artemisia and cabbage
Nasturtiums and most vegetables
Unhappy marriages
Tomatoes and beans
Sunflowers and almost anything
Cabbages and beans
Onions and peas

COMPOST

To hear compost enthusiasts talk, you'd think it was some magical substance made by alchemists, but it is only rotted vegetable matter. Yet compost is indispensable to a well-managed garden, for, whether dug into the soil or spread on it as a mulch, it replenishes the humus on which continued soil fertility depends.

Almost any kind of organic matter can be recycled into compost. That includes scraps of meat and the mice the cat keeps leaving on the back doorstep. But too much in the way of dead animals will make a foul, blowfly-infested mess, and the great bulk of the material should be of vegetable origin:

fallen leaves, grass clippings, dead cut flowers, weeds, table scraps and peelings; even shredded paper and sawdust. (Hair is innocuous; I once read of a hairdresser who composted the sweepings from her salon floor and won prizes at flower shows.)

All you have to do is gather the stuff together in a heap, and in time there will be compost, which is ready to use when it is black and crumbly, rather like a moist packeted cake mix only black; it should smell pleasant. But this can take two years, and most of the finer techniques of compost making are designed to hurry the process up. Ideally, you gather together enough material to make a heap about a metre high and a little more wide — there's no advantage in anything bigger — making sure you have a mix of coarse stuff like autumn leaves, cabbage stumps, small (non-thorny!) prunings and weeds, as well as fine stuff like grass clippings, so that the mass will neither set solid and soggy nor be too loose. Sprinkle something high in nitrogen, as an activator, on top, to get the bacteria and fungi that will do the actual fermenting started. A few handfuls of BLOOD AND BONE or poultry MANURE will do the trick, and so might the odd dead mouse, buried deep in the heap where the blowies can't get at it. You can buy 'compost activators', but they cost twice as much as blood and bone and are no more effective. Ignore the claims that they contain compost-making bacteria; no doubt they do, but any garden is already swarming with them.

As soon as fermentation starts, there will be a smell of ammonia. This shouldn't be unpleasant: if the compost heap stinks, it has got soggy. Stab it with a sharp stake in a few places to let some air in (a good idea to do this occasionally in any case). If that doesn't stop the smell in a couple of days, you may have to pull the whole thing to bits and let them dry out before reassembling them, with a sheet of plastic on top to keep the rain out.

The inside will get hot — hot enough to destroy weed seeds and diseases. It isn't wise to rely on this, though, so keep seedy weeds and oxalis

bulbs off the compost heap. And watch out for seeds in vegetable scraps — you may find many pumpkin plants popping up in unexpected places when the compost is spread. When the smell of ammonia fades — after a couple of weeks, usually — you have to decide whether to turn the heap inside out, so that the bits around the outside will get their chance to break down. (I never bother, but then I'm lazy, and I don't mind a bit of unrotted stuff in my mulches.) The compost isn't ready yet, but it's on the way; give it a few months in peace. The heap will be colonised by worms once it has cooled down; when most of them leave, the compost will be ready for use. No urgency to use it right now; it will keep for a few months.

In practice, most gardens rarely produce enough material to make a heap all at once; just add what comes to hand from time to time. There'll still be compost at the end. It's worth having three heaps, side by side: one to add to, one to take finished compost from, and one quietly maturing.

But you don't have to have a heap at all — you can simply spread what would have gone on the compost heap on your beds as a mulch. Aided by a sprinkling of blood and bone, it will rot in time. Tell anyone who remarks that kitchen scraps among the roses look untidy that you're practising 'sheet composting'.

COMPOST BINS

A spread-out compost heap rots more slowly than a compact one, and a compost bin, which is just a three-sided open box about a metre high and a little more square, is a useful thing to have. Or better, three side by side. You can make it out of bricks, with a few gaps left to let the air in, or from timber boards or logs; treated pine is good, and cedar is even more rot-proof, but it is expensive. One of the best I've ever used had simply been made by driving in four stout stakes and stapling fine-mesh chicken wire to them to make the walls. Some people like a concrete floor, but there's no need for one unless the bins are placed

where the roots of greedy trees like willows can get in to grab the compost.

You can also improvise a small bin from a plastic garbage can with some holes in it to let the air in and water out; turn the heap by shaking the bin about. Small bins mounted on a frame so that you can rotate them by a handle are available. They certainly make compost very quickly — in weeks rather than months — but in such small quantities that they fall into the category of expensive playthings in all but the tiniest of gardens.

CORM

For most gardeners, a gladiolus is a BULB but if you cut a gladiolus 'bulb' open, you won't find the intricate structure of an onion, with the growth bud buried at the base: you will find a solid mass of starch, with the growing point on top. Such a structure is called a corm; the difference is important botanically, but much less so to the gardener. A cormous

Even if you find the big flower-shop gladioli vulgar, you'll love the daintiness of 'The Bride' and the other spring-flowering gladioli. Plant their corms in autumn.

plant builds a new corm on top of the old one every year; the old one eventually rots away, or is discarded by the gardener when the gladioli are lifted, and the roots then pull the new one down to the favoured depth. As well, there are usually numbers of baby corms or cormels, sometimes so many that as they grow they crowd their parents. If you don't want to lift your gladioli each year to sort matters out, plant them deep (say 20 centimetres), so that only the biggest cormels get a chance to grow. The gladiolus's South African relatives, the freesias, sparaxis and their ilk, grow from corms, and so do CYCLAMEN and crocuses — the real ones, not the various 'autumn crocuses' (the colchicums, sternbergias and zephyranthes). For a planting guide see BULBS.

COST EFFECTIVENESS

Add up the cost of the seed, fertiliser, snail bait and what have you; the proportion of the mortgage that pays for the vegetable bed, and its share of the water rates; allow yourself a decent wage for your time — and the chances are that that home-grown lettuce will

Freesias are one of the best loved of flowers that grow from corms. To have the delightful scent at its best, forget the coloured varieties and grow this one, the old-fashioned Freesia refracta alba.

have cost you (in real terms, as economists say) more than to buy it at the greengrocer's. But what value do you place on the fact that it is absolutely fresh and on the pride of having raised it yourself? On the other hand, your time is your own, and you are paying the mortgage anyway. And will the economist with his calculator admit that no rose that you might buy at the florist is as wonderful as the one you have nourished from its infancy? In these anxious times, what price on the peace that gardens can bring to those who tend them?

But plants, fertilisers and chemicals are expensive, and the frugal gardener seeks ways to cut costs by:

◆ Buying a smaller plant rather than a larger (advanced) one.
◆ Saving one's own seeds.
◆ Exchanging cuttings with friends and neighbours.
◆ Making compost.

- Buying fertiliser and potting mix in bigger, 'economy size' bags (they keep).
- Only using chemicals when really needed, and then sparingly.
- Conserving water (see the feature on WATER and WATERING).

COTTAGE GARDENS

In the good old days — formerly known as 'these hard times' — the inhabitants of cottages usually filled their small gardens with vegetables and medicinal herbs, with only those few flowers like roses and madonna lilies that were used in folk remedies. What we think of as 'the cottage garden', with its colourful mixture of 'old fashioned', easily grown flowers and kitchen herbs, all in artless and charming disarray with roses climbing around the door, only came in with greater prosperity in the late nineteenth century, to be admired and taken up by upper-class gardeners in the reign of Edward VII.

That grand 'cottage gardens' made by people like Vita Sackville-West at Sissinghurst, in England, included plants of a rarity and costliness beyond the means of real cottagers doesn't detract from the romance of the style, which remains a delightful accompaniment to any but the most starkly modern house.

Almost any plant can be used in the cottage style, even such annuals as petunias and scarlet salvias, usually associated with municipal bedding. Just don't plant them in long rows but in clumps of half-a-dozen or so, mixed in with other plants in a grand assortment. That is what cottage gardening consists of!

Cottage garden plants
Roses, especially climbers and old-fashioned types
Carnations
Columbines
Daylilies
Lilies: November lilies, tiger lilies
Heliotrope
Irises
Daffodils
Calendulas
Herbs: rosemary, lavender, lemon thyme, bergamot
Daisies of all types
Fuchsias
Hydrangeas
Agapanthus
Red hot pokers (*Kniphofia*)
English daisies
Forget-me-nots

The cottage style at its most glorious — Monet's garden at Giverny in France.

PLANNING A CROP ROTATION

Planning a crop rotation is easy if you keep a plan of your vegetable garden. (It need not be as artistic as this!) Next year, you simply move everything down one bed. Just make sure you don't plant vegies of the same group (cabbages and cauliflowers for instance, or peas and beans) in adjacent beds.

From the top, we have marigolds, lettuces, beetroot, herbs, cabbage, onions, silverbeet, beans, capsicums, zucchini, a mix of cabbages and tomatoes, melons, peas.

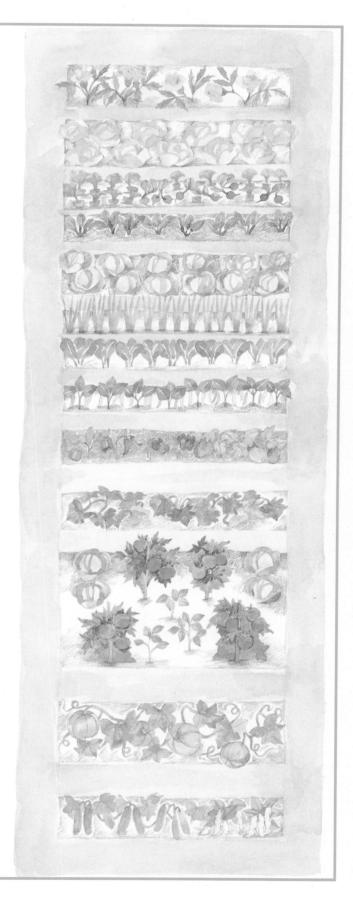

CROP ROTATION

This simply means not planting the same crop in the same place year after year, so that the soil doesn't get exhausted from yielding the same cocktail of nutrients, and soil-dwelling diseases and pests don't get a chance to build up. Thus you might follow a row of cabbages with one of carrots, then beans, lettuces, tomatoes — and then cabbages again. The idea is to follow each crop with one of a different type: roots following leaves, and in turn followed by a fruiting crop. Just which doesn't really matter, as long as you don't grow tomatoes in the same spot without a couple of years' gap (they are especially prone to VIRUSES and to NEMATODES), and make sure, for fear of club root, not to follow any of the cabbage tribe (BRASSICAS) with each other. Strawberries are also prone to viruses, and you shouldn't renew your strawberry bed in the same spot either. The inclusion of a LEGUME (beans or peas), whose roots will fix nitrogen, is desirable, but not essential. It all probably sounds more complex than it is. If you plant each type in an adjacent row, all you have to do is move the plants down one row each year, like the guests at the Mad Hatter's tea party. While the technique is most often used in the vegetable garden, where you are making the heaviest demands on the soil, it is appropriate to the flower garden too. If you have a bed where you always grow petunias, say, you might decide to grow zinnias this year, just for the change.

CROP SICKNESS

Have you ever decided to replant a rose bed and found that the new bushes simply refused to grow, even though the old ones were fine, just out of date? If you have, you've come across this problem: the soil was 'rose-sick'. It isn't only roses, though they are the commonest sufferers; orchardists have the same trouble, and it can happen with other garden plants. The tell-tale sign is the new plant's roots being black and stunted. Scientists have dignified it with the name *specific replant disease*,

but they are still largely in the dark about its cause, though it is thought that the new plants are being affected by viruses that didn't cause much worry to their predecessors. The only cure is to give the soil a rest for at least a year, possibly planting a GREEN MANURE crop or two in the meantime — practising CROP ROTATION, in fact. Replacing the soil in the bed with soil in which the plant concerned has not been grown before works too, but this is mighty hard work.

CROWN

There are two distinct meanings of crown. In the first, the crown is the ground-level part of a herbaceous plant, from which the roots grow into the ground and the leaves and flowering shoot grow up. We talk of planting delphinium, strawberry, or asparagus crowns, and take care not to plant them too deeply or bury them with mulch, lest the young shoots be smothered.

The crown can also be the array of branches and leaves carried aloft on the single stem of a tree or the several stems of a shrub. (The crown of a STANDARD plant like a standard rose is called its 'head'.) 'Raising the crown' in tree surgeon's parlance means to selectively remove some of the lower branches, to increase the headroom beneath. See PRUNING.

CULTIVAR

Time was when we used to refer to the different **varieties** of our garden plants, but the botanists have now hogged the word to mean a variety that has originated in the wild, while one created by a mere gardener must be called a **cultivar** (short for 'cultivated variety'). The distinction is not very meaningful, and insisting on it is pedantry; surely there is enough jargon in the world already.

CULTIVATION

'Excellence in cultivation' is a phrase often met with in show schedules. Here it means the whole package of skills needed to grow a plant (or an entire garden) to perfection. But the word also has the more limited meaning of disturbing the ground, by digging or hoeing, in order to loosen it up to make it more congenial for plants — we might speak of a bed as being well cultivated. While mulching, by protecting the surface soil from caking under the pressure of rain and the hose, does reduce the need for cultivation, it is still wise to do it occasionally, the best time being just before you renew the mulch.

A 'cultivated plant' is one grown in gardens, as distinct from a wild one.

CURLY LEAF

A serious disease of peaches, both fruiting and ornamental, and one that you can be fined for having in your garden. Control is by spraying the tree with a copper-based fungicide like Benlate, but by the time you see the tell-tale pink, warted leaves with their powdery bloom of fungus, it is too late: the spray *must* be applied the minute you see signs of the pink petals emerging from the baby flower buds. A follow up spray a couple of weeks later is usually advised, to be followed by picking off and burning any diseased leaves that appear.

If all you want is flowers, consider planting the equally lovely flowering almond, *Prunus pollardii,* which is much less susceptible to curly leaf.

CUT FLOWERS

If you want your flowers to last as long as possible, cut them young — not necessarily in tight bud, but before they are fully open, and in the cool of the day. Don't cut stems longer than you need, depriving the plant of foliage unnecessarily, and shorter-stemmed flowers often last longer too. Flowers with sappy stems, such as poinsettias, poppies and dahlias, need to have them cauterised by a quick dip in boiling water or a fast pass through a flame, but with most flowers it is sufficient to recut the stems under water, to prevent air bubbles from clogging their veins.

All will benefit from an hour or two in cool water up to their necks before you arrange them. Strip off all leaves that will be under water in the vase; they'll only rot and poison the water.

The vase must be scrupulously clean, the water too. People put all sorts of things in the water to prolong the lives of their flowers, from copper coins to expensive 'cut flower foods', but the best is a little fizzy, sugary soft drink — not the diet variety! Lemonade is fine, and about half a cup to the average vase (holding a litre or more) should do.

Keep the arrangement in a cool room, or at least keep it out of the sun and away from heaters. Wilted flowers can, if they aren't too far gone, often be saved by dipping the stems in boiling water for a couple of minutes, then cutting off the cooked ends and repeating the cool plunge until they recover.

CUTTINGS

A cutting is a piece of the stem of a plant, put in the ground in the hope it will make roots and grow into a new plant. Whether it be a softwood cutting taken from new growth (as with fuchsias), a semi-hardwood cutting, of growth that isn't quite mature (and usually taken in late summer, as with camellias) or a hardwood cutting, of fully matured growth in autumn or winter (roses and many trees), the gardener's job is to keep the cutting alive until the cut end calluses over and the new roots grow from the callus. Dipping the end of the cutting in rooting hormone can help the process along.

Essentially, this means keeping it moist, but not so moist that the cut end will rot, and the easiest way of doing this is to put the cuttings in a pot (old custom says around the edge) of coarsely sandy soil — poultry grit with just a little topsoil added is fine — and enclosing the whole thing in a poor man's greenhouse, alias a plastic bag. Remove any leaves that will be in the soil and trim the others in half. Softwood cuttings usually root the fastest. When the cuttings have rooted

(no harm in tipping them out of the pot after a few weeks to see), they can be put into individual pots of more fertile soil or a protected nursery bed until the new plants are big enough to plant out in their final homes.

Such plants as chrysanthemums, globe artichokes, and gazanias are propagated by cuttings of the young shoots, pulled away from the crown with a skerrick of root attached. These go by the delightfully racist name of Irishman's cuttings.

CYCLAMEN

Nothing is more tempting than a cyclamen in a florist's shop, but all too often they go into decline the minute you get them home. They aren't at all easy to please, needing to be kept fairly cool, and in a humid atmosphere, and

they are very prone to rot if the CROWN gets damp. So don't heat your room to more than about 16–18°C; put the plant on a saucer of wet pebbles (as with AFRICAN VIOLETS); and keep the crown dry. Don't water the foliage; to water, stand the pot in a basin of water for half an hour, once or twice a week. Pull the spent flowers away gently and cleanly, leaving no stub of stalk to rot. If the plant survives to die down naturally for the summer, keep it bone dry until it starts to show signs of life in the autumn; then it can be repotted in fresh soil and the whole cycle begun again. Gloxinias are treated similarly.

As well as the florist's cyclamen, bred from *Cyclamen persicum*, there are some enchanting miniature species for cool climate gardens; they prefer a shady spot. The autumn-flowering *C. hederaefolium* is the best known.

The florist's cyclamen comes in a wide variety of colours, but rarely has the scent of the wild species (Cyclamen persicum) from which it is derived. It will grow outdoors in a mild-winter climate.

DECIDUOUS

Quite apart from any autumn fireworks they may stage, deciduous trees and vines perform the useful trick of providing shade in summer but not in winter when it is less welcome. But they vary a bit in their timetable, some dropping their leaves earlier in the autumn and leafing out later in the spring than others. This may be a factor worth considering in your choice of species if you are planning to use deciduous trees to shade the house. Raking up fallen leaves is a chore, but don't fall into the common error of thinking that evergreens don't drop leaves — they do, one by one; usually in the spring and sometimes for months. You might find the all-at-once autumn drop less of a bother.

DESIGN

It is in the initial stages of garden making, when you lay out the garden and landscape your plot (considering such things as sun and shade, places for children to play, and where the vegetable plot will go), that design is your chief activity, but you are still designing every time you plant something or prune a plant to shape. No need to be self-conscious about it; gardeners soon acquire the designer's instinctive concern that, whatever they are doing, the result should look good.

But sometimes we forget, allowing our desire for some new plant to override our judgment that it doesn't

really fit the style of the garden or even look good with its neighbours. There's no shame in making mistakes — all gardeners do. Vita Sackville-West once said that half the art of making a beautiful garden was having the courage to abolish ugly and unsuccesful plants. And if you can't bear to destroy a mistake, pot it up and give it away.

DIE BACK
see PHYTOPHTHORA

DIGGING

Whether, in preparing the soil for planting, you dig it over with a spade or a fork is a matter of preference. A spade does turn the soil over more thoroughly, but in ground that has already been cultivated I prefer a fork: it is marginally less heavy to use and won't cut any forgotten bulbs in half. But I should prefer a spade if there are likely to be roots from trees or shrubs, as it's better to cut them cleanly than tear them about. Digging is hard work, made even harder if your soil is either caked dry by drought or sodden with rain; the best time is a day or two after rain or watering, when the soil is still just nicely damp.

Digging to the full depth of the blade (a spade's depth) is only for empty ground; cultivation among established plantings can only be about half as deep, or even less, for most plants have their feeding roots rather close to the surface; here a small hand fork is the best tool.

Nature doesn't dig, relying on worms and other underground creatures to keep the soil aerated and to draw down the nutrients from the decay of plants and animal matter that she leaves to lie on the surface. We can imitate her in the garden by mulching and growing carpets of leafy plants, but the ecology of a garden remains an artificial one: some CULTIVATION is still needed from time to time.

DISBUDDING

Removing some of a plant's flower buds, in the hope that it will concentrate its energy in a few large blooms, rather than dissipating it in many little ones, is known as disbudding. Chrysanthemum fanciers often disbud drastically, leaving only three or four buds on the plant; the result is the colossal blooms that you see at shows and in flower shops. It is usually a good idea to remove the very first flower bud (the **crown bud**) that appears on such plants as chrys-anthemums, dahlias, zinnias or marigolds, to encourage branching and more flowers, and camellias sometimes set more buds than they can open properly, but with most plants the operation is entirely optional.

DISBUDDING

1 *Camellias tend to make clusters of buds, often more than the plant can open properly.*

2 *Reducing the clusters to single buds (pairs at most) gives each the chance to develop to perfection. Disbud as soon as the buds are large enough to handle, in mid-autumn.*

DIVISION

Clumpy perennial plants are easily propagated by division at the usual planting time, that is late autumn through spring. Sometimes the clump will simply fall into pieces once you have dug it up and shaken the soil from the roots, but often you have to force it apart. Tradition calls for two forks thrust in the middle, back to back, and levered apart, but you can also simply cut the crown in pieces with secateurs, provided that you go gently. (This isn't very good for your best pair of secateurs!) Little is to be gained by cutting a clump into tiny pieces: it's better to accept fewer but more substantial new plants, discarding old, worn-out bits from the centre of the clump. Strelitzias can be divided, but the crowns are massive and go deep; Irishman's CUTTINGS are easier.

Clumps of bulbs usually come apart easily; if you have to cut an offset away from its parent bulb, it's usually too small to leave home.

Dahlia fanciers like to take out the first flower bud that appears (the 'crown bud'), and then the side buds on the shoots that follow, for this result — large, long-stemmed flowers.

DIVISION

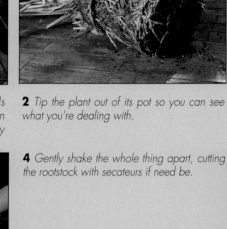

1 *While some of the more exotic orchids need special treatment, overgrown cymbidiums can be divided like any herbaceous plant.*

2 *Tip the plant out of its pot so you can see what you're dealing with.*

3 *Dead and worn-out bits from the middle of the clump should be discarded.*

4 *Gently shake the whole thing apart, cutting the rootstock with secateurs if need be.*

5 *The result — several healthy new plants. Don't try to get too many; larger divisions grow faster and flower sooner.*

DOUBLE DIGGING

This isn't just digging over a bed twice: it is a way of cultivating the soil more deeply than a spade can normally reach. Start by making a trench to the width and depth of your spade (one spit deep) at one end of your bed, barrowing the topsoil you take out down to the other. Then dig over the subsoil at the bottom of your trench, digging in as much compost, rotted manure or the like as you have, but leaving the dug-over soil in place, to receive the topsoil from the second, adjacent trench thrown in on top of it, maybe with more compost in-corporated with it too, and so on to the end, when the very last trench is filled with the reserved soil from the first one — after which you stagger off for a cup of tea and a massage for your aching back.

DOUBLES

A double flower is simply one that has more than its natural complement of petals; a wild rose or carnation, for instance, has only five, a garden variety might have as many as seventy. The wild, five-petalled flower would be described as **single;** one with more, but fewer than it might have (say a rose with about fifteen) as **semi-double.**

'Pascali', with about 30 petals, is a double-flowered rose.

Planting

Planting may be the most important single job in gardening — after all, if you don't plant, you'll never get any results — but it's also one of the easiest. In principle, all you have to do is make a hole, put the roots in it, fill back the soil around them, and water to settle everything in. But, like children, plants appreciate a good start in life, and it's well worth taking a little trouble over planting.

First, make sure your planting spot has been well dug over, so that the soil is nice and crumbly (in good tilth) to allow the new roots to grow into it. If the soil is settled and firm, the roots may be reluctant (particularly in heavy soils) to grow out beyond the soft soil in the planting hole. So CULTIVATE as large an area as you can, preferably the whole bed. This needn't wait until planting day. If you can prepare the soil a couple of weeks before, so much the better: you can then dig in some COMPOST or MANURE and give it time to lose any rawness it might have. In dry weather, a thorough watering a day or two ahead will ensure that you are planting into moist soil. The plant itself should be watered before you plant it; if its root ball is dry, the plant can be reluctant to absorb water after it is planted, and the root ball more likely to fall apart in handling.

Ideally, you should make your planting hole, plant your plant, and water it in all in one operation, but sometimes (as when you're planting a rose bed for example) it's convenient to make the holes in advance. No harm will come if the hole sits open for a few hours, but a lapse of several days will allow the sides to dry out and settle, and if it rains the whole affair may end up in a mess.

Don't, the old saying has it, waste a ten-dollar plant in a one-dollar hole! Not only does a stingy hole make it harder to manoeuvre your plant, you give it less freshly cultivated soil immediately next to its roots.

Once the ground is prepared, it's then a matter of taking the plant from its container, disturbing its roots as little as possible, and placing it in the hole, adding soil beneath it if need be so that it won't end up any deeper than before. Don't, please, pick the plant up by its stem, as you run the risk of the weight of the soil damaging the roots. Hold it by the root ball, and if that is big and heavy, make a cradle with an old sack and call on a second pair of hands. Then fill in around it, water it in thoroughly, and the job is done. If you are planning to mulch, placing the MULCH is the last step.

Nurseries normally grow plants in soil mixes that are lighter and more open than most garden soils, and plants are sometimes reluctant to send their roots out into the more solid garden soil. It is, therefore, wise to add some sand and maybe a little compost to the soil with which you backfill your planting holes, to create a transition zone.

The procedure is the same for any plant with soil around its roots. For BARE ROOT plants like roses or fruit trees see that entry. Bare-rooted PERENNIALS just get placed in their hole with the soil gently placed around them, and bulbs are simplicity itself: just sit them on the bottom of the hole and put the soil back, turning the sprinkler on the whole planting when you've finished.

PLANTING SEEDLINGS

1 *Seedlings often come in punnets of six. If they come in plastic pots rather like egg cartons, cut them into individual pots and then give them the upside-down treatment.*

2 *The easiest way to get the seedlings out is to tip the punnet upside down the way you do with a pot.*

1 To remove a plant from a pot, turn it upside down, cradling the roots in your hand, and give the pot a sharp tap on the rim. It will then lift off and the plant is ready to turn right way up for planting.

3 With the soil filled in around, the plant is in its new home, sitting no deeper than it was in the pot. (If you made the hole too deep, just put a bit of soil in the bottom.)

2 Never pick up a plant by the stem, in its pot or out of it — the weight of the soil can tear the roots. Planting from a pot is easy: just make an appropriate sized hole and put the plant in it.

3 Gently separate the seedlings. If the roots are tangled (as is often the case) it can be difficult to avoid losing soil, and then it is better to cut them apart with a kitchen knife.

4 Plant very slightly deeper than they were in the punnet (it helps to keep them from falling over), firming them gently in place with your fingers. When all the seedlings are in, water gently.

'Mermaid' is often thought to be the most beautiful of all single roses.

Native to the semi-desert countries of the Middle East, bearded irises (this is 'Camelot Rose') are wonderful plants for the water-thrifty gardener — they actually like being allowed to dry out in summer. (New growth comes with the autumn rains.)

The extra petals are normally formed at the expense of stamens, and thus a double-flowered plant is likely to be more-or-less sterile. Often, as with stocks, it will be completely so. Since stocks are grown from seed, which must perforce be taken from single-flowered plants, there will always be a percentage of 'singles' among the seedlings; a good seedsman tries to select strains so that singles will be as few as possible .

Sometimes this sterility is an advantage. The ordinary gorse (*Ulex europaeus*) is a dreadful weed, but the owner of the double version can enjoy its sweet fragrance without worry.

Double flowers are often showier and longer-lasting than singles.

DROUGHT

The trouble with droughts, weather forecasters notwithstanding, is that they don't give advance warning of their coming: it hasn't rained for weeks, and suddenly a drought is on. If you have been prepared, with your garden deeply watered and well mulched, you can ride out a short drought, watering only the plants in most urgent need and relying on the others to keep sending their roots deeper to where there is still moisture. But when you water, the old

rule applies: give plenty but infrequently. Any old country gardener will tell you that it is better to harden your heart and not water at all than to tease the plants into keeping their roots near the surface.

A drought-stricken tree is a sad sight, but don't sprinkle it; just leave a hose dribbling at its roots for a long time — overnight at least, preferably for twenty-four hours. Trees often suffer more from a wet season following a drought than from the drought itself, because they make more growth than their drought-damaged roots can handle when the rain starts. Judicious pruning and thinning of the foliage can save the day.

DROUGHT-TOLERANT PLANTS

It is a bit misleading to describe a plant as drought-tolerant as though that were something built into it by nature: so much depends on the usual wetness of the climate. An ancient camellia may indeed have survived long dry spells in Sydney's humid climate, but take it to

Gazanias are excellent plants for growing in seaside gardens, whose sandy soil dries out so rapidly in summer; but they enjoy dry climates inland too.

Regular crepe myrtles will grow to 5 or 6 metres tall; the newish dwarf strains make dome shaped bushes, only a metre or so tall — even less with hard pruning.

the dry inland, and it will have a hard time coping even with a normal summer there. Conversely, a species used to low rainfall and dryness in the air may languish in a humid coastal climate, even in a dry season.

A look around the neighbourhood during the next long dry spell will give you a pretty good idea of what plants will flourish on your local rainfall. I'll bet that among them will be some of great beauty — good enough to form the backbone of your plantings.

DWARF

'Dwarf' might suggest a plant of very low stature, suitable for admiration by a garden gnome, but usually all it means is that the plant is rather lower growing than usual. Many of the dwarf conifers are indeed miniatures, but other dwarfs can still be quite large. The 'dwarf' lemon-scented gum (*Eucalyptus citriodora* 'Compacta'), at 8 or 10 metres tall is so only by comparison with the normal species, which grows to 30 metres or more. With the ever-decreasing size of modern gardens, dwarf varieties are often thought more suitable, but are they really? One

wouldn't put half-size furniture in a small living room — and surely much of the beauty of, say, a snapdragon is lost when its majestic spikes of flowers are compressed into solitary blooms on a ground-hugging plant?

Old gardening books often refer to dwarf roses (sometimes to dwarf fruit trees also), but what they mean are ordinary rosebushes (as opposed to STANDARDS).

EARTHING UP

To get nice white stalks on things like asparagus and celery — to BLANCH them — you have to exclude the light from them altogether. Traditionally this is done by heaping up earth around them a week or two before harvest, either by 'borrowing' the necessary earth from nearby in the bed or by wheeling in some sand or soil from elsewhere. You don't have to shovel soil: try bundling your celery stalks in a straitjacket of heavy paper or black plastic. It's all a bit of a chore, and adds to the cost of the vegetable in the shop, which is why we usually see green asparagus and celery in the markets these days.

EDGES AND EDGING

We sometimes talk of a ribbon of low plants 'edging' a bed of taller ones, as with lobelias in front of marigolds, but usually we are thinking of the edge of the lawn that fronts the bed. Trimming edges is a tedious job, but essential if the lawn isn't to look neglected and

EPIPHYTES

An epiphyte is a plant that grows away from the soil, usually in the branches of a tree, but doesn't draw nourishment from its host (in which case it would be a *parasite,* and probably a pest). The staghorn fern is a familiar example, and is almost always grown attached to a tree trunk. Most orchids, BROMELIADS, and some cacti (the epiphyllums and their kind) are epiphytes too, and when we grow these in pots, they need to be given a very loose, leafy potting mix and perfect drainage.

A tree laden with blossoming orchids can be quite a sight, and a great conversation piece. It's not at all difficult to do. Choose species suited to your climate (a specialist nursery or a good orchid book can offer guidance);

Victorian-style terracotta edging tiles are used here to trim the brick paving around the weeping standard rose. (It is the variety 'Sea Foam'.)

edges is a tedious job, but essential if the lawn isn't to look neglected and scruffy. A strip of bricks or concrete on which one wheel of the mower can ride can largely eliminate the task, at the price of destroying any effect of naturalness you might be trying to achieve with your planting. Bricks are

less assertive than the white of concrete, though this can always be coloured (add manganese dioxide to the wet concrete for dark grey). Victorian gardens often featured fancy terracotta edging tiles, now available again, or bricks laid at an angle for a sawtooth effect, but these catch the mower; in the old days they were used to hold the junction between flowers and gravel.

Bricks laid flat help eliminate hand-trimming of the edges of the lawn; here they also reinforce the formal lines of the plantings.

attach the plants to the tree with nylon fishing line (which doesn't rot and is practically invisible); and pack a couple of handfuls of sphagnum moss or orchid compost around each plant. The orchids will need regular watering and the occasional splash of MANURE WATER. Take care in setting plants in forks, as you won't want to encourage rot in your tree. A not-too-shady, rough-barked tree is best; orchid growers swear by casuarinas.

ESPALIER

The original purpose in training fruit trees, especially apples, pears and peaches, flat against walls was to encourage early ripening of the fruit by the extra warmth reflected from the

A fruit tree, espaliered in the traditional formal manner against a brick wall. Later in the summer, the new branches at the top will be bent horizontally to continue the pattern.

These epiphytic bromeliads are growing on a dead tree in a greenhouse — but the idea works even better on a living tree in the garden.

masonry. Now that we can have most fruit from cold storage the year round, we train plants to *espalier* mainly for decorative effect, and don't limit ourselves just to fruit trees. Hibiscus, camellias (especially sasanquas), the ravishingly scented *Philadelphus mexicanus*, or indeed any shrub that can tolerate regular discipline, can all be trained to slip-cover a wall or fence, and in a limited space may well prove easier to manage than true climbing plants with their more rampant growth.

The effect can be deliciously formal or one of studied casualness; either way it is not at all difficult to achieve. First, you need to fix a trellis, or at least a series of horizontal wires about 35 centimetres apart, to the wall. Then it is just a matter of planting your chosen plant, tying in the shoots that can be bent to meet the trellis, and cutting back any that can't, as well as any that might interfere with your chosen pattern. When the available space is filled up — which is likely to take at least a couple of years — pruning will just consist of removing unwanted shoots at the appropriate pruning time.

EVERGREENS

An evergreen doesn't hold its leaves forever; eventually each leaf does fall, but not before new ones have taken its place, so that there are leaves on the plant all the time. Evergreen trees and shrubs are the first choice for building the basic form of the garden, and especially for blotting out unwanted views, but deciduous species can still hold the eye too, if their branches are dense enough. And where you face the common problem of the hot sun and a desirable view in the same direction, deciduous species can be the best choice: you at least have the pleasure of the view in winter when the leaves have fallen.

Almost all Australian and New Zealand plants are evergreen, and evergreens from other countries enjoy our mild climates, but gardeners in very cold climates have a more restricted choice, having to rely largely on conifers — the pines and their relatives — whose character is very different from the broad-leafed plants.

FANCY NAMES

There is a current fashion among nurseries for replacing both the botanical and the accepted English names with catchy new ones, such as Pharaoh's Daughter for *Cissus rhomboidea* 'Ellen Danica', which is a fancy-leaved kangaroo vine, or Summer Love for a dwarf species of *Acalypha*. But one could wish for it to pass; such

names may help sales, but they make it very difficult to look the plant up in books to find out how to grow it.

The names of CULTIVARS are a different matter: we expect to be told that the shrub with red flowers is a camellia before we learn that it is the variety called 'The Czar'. The customary use of quotation marks avoids confusion, as in "The Czarina won first prize at the St Petersburg flower show with 'The Czar'."

FIRE IN THE GARDEN

'Burning off' — the old bushie's trick of clearing unwanted vegetation by setting it on fire — might have its place in primitive agriculture, but it has none in the suburban garden. Much less dangerous to pull out the weeds or whatever and put them on the compost heap, or in the incinerator to be burned there. The incinerator (you will have a hose nearby, in case of unforeseen disaster, won't you?) remains the best way of disposing of garden rubbish that is too weedy, diseased, woody, or thorny to be trusted to the compostheap, and the resulting ASH is useful fertiliser. But not valuable COMPOST material like fallen leaves and grass clippings, please!

It has now been discovered that backyard burning is one of the major causes of dirty air in our cities, and more and more suburban councils are banning the incinerator, forcing us to take our uncompostable rubbish to the tip, there to create pollution of a different kind.

FLOWERING TREES

Just about all trees bear flowers, though in many cases they aren't very conspicuous, but many are grown for their bright display of blossoms — think of jacarandas, bauhinias, the Illawarra flame tree, magnolias, and the 'flowering' fruit trees, such as peaches, plums, apricots, cherries. These last are bred for ornament rather than their fruit, which is inferior in quality, but the regular fruiting varieties are beautiful in blossom too, and if you are going to have to spray your trees against pests and diseases you might prefer to have fruit as well as blossoms for your trouble.

The 'flowering cabbage' is not a tree, but neither is it grown for its flowers, rather for its gorgeously coloured leaves, which are as edible as ordinary cabbage and make quite nice, if odd-looking, coleslaw. Like most annuals, it likes sun and rich soil.

F1 HYBRIDS

F1 is plant breeder's shorthand for *first filial generation*. F1 hybrid seed is the result of carefully crossing two very pure strains of the plant in question to achieve both hybrid vigour (see XENIA) and great uniformity of habit, flower or general quality in the resulting offspring in your garden. In the next generation (F2), anything might happen, which is why it is useless saving the seed from such hybrids yourself — they don't 'breed true'.

Most strains of annuals (just about all petunias and marigolds) and many vegetables are F1 hybrids these days.

FRAGRANCE
see NIGHT-SCENTED FLOWERS, SCENT

The Japanese cherry 'Shirotae', which is also known as 'Mt Fuji', appears in its full spring glory, with autumn colour to follow. No fruit — but then fruiting cherries need a colder winter than this one does.

FROST

Nature is an economical lady. If a living creature doesn't need some feature to survive in its environment, it doesn't evolve it, which is why we don't have feathers, and why plants native to places where frost doesn't occur have no ability to cope with being frozen. Even plants that can cope with frost vary in their hardiness — they don't all come from homelands with equally severe winters.

Plant sap is mostly water, and thus it expands as it freezes. The resulting pressure can rupture the cell walls. If a plant is designed to resist frost, it can either develop strong cell walls, or, as winter approaches, concentrate its sap so that its freezing point is as low as possible, providing itself with insulation, in the form of bark, the waxy scales that cover the growth buds of deciduous trees, or the thick surfaces of evergreen leaves. (Deciduous plants sidestep the issue of protecting their leaves by shedding them in autumn or by dying down to roots or bulbs that are safe beneath the soil; pines have resinous sap that has to get very cold before it freezes.)

Should freezing weather occur early, before the plant is ready, or unexpectedly late, after sappy new growth has started, there will be trouble. This is why gardeners (wine-growers especially) fear late spring frosts and avoid giving fertiliser late in the growing season lest young growth that won't be mature in time be encouraged. It takes time for a plant to actually freeze, and thus one that can put up with a short frost might well be damaged in a prolonged one.

If a plant is on the borderline of hardiness in your climate, there are ways of helping it out. You might grow it in a pot, bringing it indoors or into a greenhouse for the winter; you might grow it in a warm spot, such as against a sunny wall that will radiate the sun's warmth during the night; or you might give a herbaceous plant a blanket of mulch to protect its crown. Often you only have to keep the plant a couple of degrees warmer than it would otherwise be to tip the scales in its favour.

It is an old rule never to site a tender plant where the first rays of the morning sun can reach it — the rapid thawing that results can be more damaging than the slow freezing of the night before.

It would take a whole book to list frost-tender and frost-resistant plants, and it wouldn't be a great help, because conditions vary so much over the country. Local knowledge (consult a local nursery) and looking at what flourishes in gardens in your area are the best guides.

FRUIT FLY

Beloved of geneticists because its genes can be easily studied and manipulated in the laboratory, the fruit fly *Drosophila melanogaster* and its Australian cousins are much less popular with gardeners — and with the Department of Agriculture, which can take you to court for harbouring them. The fly lays her eggs on half-grown fruit — most commonly stone fruit, but also on citrus, tomatoes and capsicums — and by the time the fruit is ripe, it is ruined by being full of little white worms.

The only real control is regular spraying with a systemic insecticide like Rogor or Lebaycid, which the plant absorbs, making it poisonous to insects — and to people too; you can't spray within a fortnight or so before harvest. (Follow the directions on the bottle carefully.) If you don't like the idea you can try a poison bait that you brush on the tree, or a baited trap (a popular brand used to have the name 'Dak-pot'), but they are nothing like as effective, and the safe insecticides like

Fruit fly, bane of the backyard fruit grower.

pyrethrum and tobacco water even less so. Any infected fruit *must* be destroyed, either by burning it or boiling it up, after which you can put the mess on the compost heap.

FUNGI

Mushrooms are fungi, and there are many plants that need to have certain fungi (called mycorrhizal fungi) growing around their roots to flourish, but the fungi of most concern to gardeners and farmers are the pathogenic fungi that cause most plant diseases. Fungi, like the many kinds of MILDEW, that attack leaves, shoots or fruits are mostly easy enough to control by timely application of a suitable fungicide, bought at the local garden centre. (Take the garden centre's advice on the best ones for the problem, and follow the directions on the box to the letter.) Fungi that infect roots — most important are PHYTOPHTHORA and HONEY FUNGUS — are much more difficult to deal with; fortunately they are much less common.

GARDENIAS

There are several species of gardenia, some of them small subtropical trees, but all have scented white flowers. The most popular is the gardenia of the florist's shop, *Gardenia jasminoides*, with its DOUBLE flowers and exotic fragrance. It is a plant for a warm, humid climate, objecting to more than the faintest frost (the little creeping variety 'Radicans' is the hardiest), and, though not desperately lime-hating, is

apt to suffer from shortage of IRON in alkaline soil. The bush often goes chlorotic (that is, the leaves turn yellow) in the spring, due to a shortage of magnesium, but don't rush to give it epsom salts unless the problem stays after the weather warms up properly. Otherwise, gardenias will give no trouble in a humus-rich soil and light shade. They make pleasant temporary indoor plants while they are in bloom.

Gardenia leaves are rich, dark green, the better to show off the waxy whiteness of the flowers. If yours stay palish or yellowish in summer, the plant is calling for some fertiliser

GARLIC

The king of herbs can be used, fresh, as a vegetable — have you ever tried forty-garlic chicken? (Just peel forty garlic cloves, stuff the chicken with them, and roast; the flavour is wonderfully delicate.)

Garlic is very easy to grow. Buy a couple of knobs of garlic from the greengrocer's in early spring, separate them into cloves, and plant them about 10 centimetres apart in the vegetable garden. They will be ready to dig up in autumn when the leaves wither, and in the meantime you can judiciously harvest the leaves to add a mild garlic flavour to cooking.

Garlic is also said to repel aphids from plants nearby (see COMPANION PLANTS).

Garlic water is a popular insecticide with organic gardeners. It is made by crushing three or four cloves of garlic and infusing them in a bit more than half a litre of hot water. (You can make it stronger if you like.) When it is cool and strongly smelling of garlic, strain and spray the aphids with it.

GLYPHOSATE

The stuff of gardeners' dreams: an effective weed poisoner that doesn't poison the soil. Sold under such names as 'Zero' and 'Roundup', it works by preventing the plant from absorbing moisture, so it dies of thirst in a few days — hence its generic title of **desiccant weed-killer.** It isn't selective, so you must be careful not to spray it on any plant you don't want to kill; in close country you can paint it on with a small paintbrush. (If you do happen to brush a wanted leaf accidentally, cut it off before harm can be done.) It is most effective in hot weather, and on difficult cases like nutgrass you may need to repeat the dose. The stuff is poisonous; take the usual precautions (see the feature on SAFETY IN THE GARDEN).

CLEFT GRAFTING, THE BASIC METHOD

1 *First cut off the stock where you want the graft to go, and split it right across. Then prepare the scion, trimming it to a long wedge shape to fit the cleft.*

2 *Insert the scions, one on either side of the cleft, making sure the green cambium layers just below the bark match up perfectly. Wedging the cleft open allows you freedom of movement without damaging anything.*

3 *Once the scions are in place, remove the wedge, bind everything tight wih raffia, and coat the graft with grafting wax to keep the sap in and the rain out.*

ssep

GRAFTING

Grafting is the marrying of a *scion*—- a piece of branch — to an UNDERSTOCK (or just stock), which provides the roots, usually more vigorous or disease-resistant ones than the scion would make for itself (but see UNDERSTOCK). There are several ways of effecting the union — cleft grafting, approach grafting or inarching, bud grafting or budding — but all need exquisite care in ensuring that the cambium layers (the fine band of green immediately below the bark) come perfectly into contact, and that the scion doesn't dry out. Fruit and other deciduous trees that are grafted in late winter can be kept sufficiently protected by dolloping grafting wax (not the easiest substance to come by, but a good nursery should be able to get it for you) over the union; a spring or summer graft can be enclosed in a polythene bag to make a temporary mini-greenhouse and given some SHADING. See also BUDDING.

GREEN FINGERS

That some people have a seemingly magical ability to make any plant flourish under their care has been known for ages, but are green fingers really so inexplicable? Is it not simply that their lucky owner has an instinctive understanding that plants are living things needing care, and takes the trouble to give it to them?

And yet, we don't really understand what life is; it may indeed be that plants can sense that their owner loves them and respond accordingly, as people do.

GREEN MANURE

Green manure isn't the dung of environmentally conscious animals; the term is a holdover from the days when 'manure' meant anything that was dug into the soil to improve it. It refers to the practice of growing a crop of a leafy plant which is dug in to the ground at maturity, there to rot and make humus. It is still a valuable way to prepare new soil, or to refresh ground that has been cropped with vegetables or flowers for some time; though it does mean taking

time out for the green manure crop to grow. LEGUMES, which contribute the nitrogen fixed on their roots, are the most valuable. Clover, lucerne (alfalfa) or a cheap strain of annual lupin can all be used, and old-fashioned gardeners swear by potatoes for 'cleaning' a weedy patch of ground. The tops, which grow so thick they smother the weeds, are dug in when the potatoes are harvested. Never mind the strange looks from the neighbours when they see a (temporary) potato patch on the site of the future front lawn and shrubbery.

GROUNDCOVERS

Lawn is a groundcover, but the term (which comes to us from the United States) usually means a permanent planting of vigorous but low-growing plants that cover the ground with a carpet of foliage to smother weeds and look pretty; the fact that you generally can't walk on them won't matter if they are thoughtfully placed in the garden layout.

Such things as ivy, prostrate junipers, *Vinca minor*, *Hypericum*, and some of the ground-hugging grevilleas like 'Royal Mantle' are popular for the

Groundcovers are normally perennial plants, but nasturtiums are delightful for quick, cheap cover — and in mild climates they will self-sow for years.

A green-manure crop of clover, ready to be dug in when it comes into full flower. A second crop can follow if you have time for it.

purpose, but there are many, many others to choose from, varying in their needs for sun, shade, and water — and in their ability to crowd out the weeds too, a point to watch. Groundcovers can be labour saving, but only once they are established! In the early stages, you have to take as much trouble over them as with any other plants. Prepare the soil as usual, taking particular care to start with weed-free ground or there will be trouble later.

The plants need to be set fairly close, usually not more than 30 centimetres each way for reasonably fast results, and this can lead to the need for prodigious numbers of them; economy will usually dictate that you buy them small or propagate them yourself. Keep the spaces between the plants weeded until the cover is complete (a mulch is a great help here) and water and fertilise as needed. It can be tempting to create patterns with different plants, but choose carefully: unless you intervene fairly frequently the more vigorous growers will eventually take over the planting. Eventually you may find an annual haircut desirable; immediately after flowering is usually the appropriate time. Otherwise, all the care needed should be watering in summer and a light fertilising in spring, before growth starts. Most ground cover plants (the good ones, anyway) are pretty easy-going.

The upside-down orchid, Stanhopea tigrina, flourishing in a wire hanging basket. Wire baskets last longer than willow ones, but you need to line them to keep the potting mix in. Nurseries sell coconut-fibre liners, or you can pack around the basket with sphagnum moss. Strips of bark from that gum tree that is always shedding all over the lawn can be used too.

HANGING BASKETS

A hanging basket or pot can be a delightful way to show off a trailing plant like a fuchsia, a variegated ivy, a cascading fern (the list is endless), and can be a good way to make EPIPHYTES like orchids feel at home. Indeed, the fascinating upside-down orchid (*Stanhopea*) must be grown in a basket if you are ever to see its flowers, which grow downwards through the soil to emerge below the roots. In nature, it grows on the branches of trees. But being raised aloft in every breeze, baskets dry out quickly and any plant in a basket will need more frequent watering than it would in a conventional, ground-level pot. Check both the basket and the means by which it is suspended regularly — the plant may well be ruined if it falls.

Plants suitable for hanging baskets
Fuchsias
Ivy geraniums
Ivy, in all its pretty
variegated varieties
Nasturtiums
Petunias
Busy Lizzie (*Impatiens*)
Pendulous-flowered tuberous begonias
Most ferns
Azaleas
Orchids
Herbs

HARDINESS

'They'll be all right, they're pretty hardy,' said a clumsy friend by way of an excuse for stepping on my petunias. But 'hardy' doesn't really mean tough and easy to grow (much less being able to put up with abuse like that!). Its strict meaning is that the plant so described is able to endure a certain amount of cold and frost. We might say that a plant is hardy to zero, to minus 15°C, meaning that is the lowest temperature that it can stand without being killed or at least crippled.

The US Department of Agriculture has produced a map of 'hardiness zones' for the United States, based on the minimum winter temperatures expected in the various parts of the country, and American writers frequently describe a plant as 'hardy to zone 8' or 6 or whatever. Hardiness zones have been worked out for Europe too, but would be of little use for Australia, where our limiting factors are more usually heat and drought rather than cold.

HEDGES

A hedge is simply a row of shrubs, closely spaced so that they grow together in a solid mass. Whether you clip them to a formal shape or allow them to grow freely, with only occasional pruning to keep them bushy to the ground, will depend on your taste and the style of your garden. Ankle-high clipped hedges, of box, rosemary, or lavender, are used to edge flowerbeds in very formal gardens in the French or Italian styles (see PARTERRES); tall hedges, clipped or not, are used for privacy or to divide the garden into rooms.

There is no need to limit your choice to privet; let your imagination be your guide. Any bushy shrubs that can take regular pruning can be used — though if you plan to clip, those with fairly small leaves will look less mutilated. You can even make tall hedges with trees that will stand the constant curtailment: yew and cypress are common, and hawthorn hedges, their branches woven together basket-

Admiring Camellia japonica *for its flowers, we don't usually think of it as material for formal hedges, but its naturally slow, compact growth makes it very suitable. This camellia hedge is in the garden of the Imperial Palace in Tokyo. Clipped after bloom each year, it still flowers well.* Camellia sasanqua *is faster growing and smaller in leaf.*

wise (**laid**) to make them impenetrable, used to be a feature of the English countryside before modern agriculture started sweeping them away. But in the average garden, shrubs are safer and less work.

A clipped **tapestry hedge**, with the foliage of two or more different plants woven together, can be a pleasing feature. You might try blending *Murraya paniculata* with *Viburnum tinus*, perhaps adding the red young leaves of a photinia for further richness, but take care not to overdo it.

To make a clipped hedge, first prepare your soil well, then put your plants in at perhaps a third of the spacing you would normally use: for a box edging, about 30 centimetres apart, for a head-high hedge of plants such as rhamnus or *Camellia sasanqua*, a metre or so. Stake the plants if needed, and water and fertilise as usual.

It is tempting to encourage the plants to grow up to their final height as quickly as possible, but you must be patient and keep the plants bushy by pruning their flanks. If you let them get leggy and bare at the base now, it will be difficult to persuade them to fill in later. Once the final size is reached, it is just a matter of clipping. Then you will be glad of your patience in choosing a fairly slow-growing plant — rapid growers like privet need constant discipline.

To rejuvenate an old, overgrown hedge, just cut it back ruthlessly to its proper shape and give it some water and fertiliser; new growth will soon take away the butchered look. But be careful: some conifers, notably cypresses, won't grow back if you cut into old wood, and with them you may be better off grubbing out the whole thing and starting again.

Pottering in a greenhouse

In a mild climate, a greenhouse is something of a luxury, but as with so many luxuries, once you've indulged, you may find yourself wondering how you ever did without it. A greenhouse allows you to start seeds and cuttings early and in a controlled environment; to grow tropical plants that suffer from cold even where there mightn't be actual frost; to have ordinary garden plants like roses or tomatoes out of season; and it can be a resting place for indoor plants that are tired of the living-room.

A greenhouse needn't be very large. You can cram in a lot of plants, and start a lot of cuttings, in a space two metres by three, or even two by two and a half. As long as it gets the sun for at least half the day, you can place a greenhouse to suit the design of the garden. It could be a focal point, or you may think that unless you go in for an ornamental Victorian-style structure, a greenhouse won't be much to look at from outside. You could also attach it to the house as a conservatory — when it could be grand enough to serve as an extra living-room or even to house a spa bath. (But, if you do this make sure you can close off the conservatory, and its warmth and humidity, from the rest of the house.)

A GREENHOUSE FROM A KIT

The easiest way to acquire a greenhouse is to buy one of the standard assemble-it-yourself models, where all you have to provide is the foundations. These structures are usually made of aluminium and just bolt together. Check what optional extras are available: they might include extra benches and automated watering systems. Heating is rarely a necessity in Australia, but if you live in one of the colder parts of the country and want to grow really tropical things, it can be a comfort to know that you can keep the temperature from falling below about 10°C. The greenhouse makers usually offer heating as an option, or you might consider adapting a small reverse-cycle air conditioner, like those made for caravans, and running it on a thermostat. If you are offered extra ventilators, take them: it's fatally easy to allow the temperature to shoot up in summer and turn your greenhouse into a Turkish bath, and the more fresh air you can get to your plants the better.

SHADING

Make sure the design allows you to attach SHADECLOTH for the summer; commercial tomato growers whitewash the glass in spring, relying on the rain to wash it off by the end of autumn, but this looks dreadful in the garden. You might be offered the choice of having glass right to ground level, or just to that of the potting bench, with brick or timber below that. I should prefer the full height glass; there'll then be enough light to grow things under the bench, or to put pots of cuttings there. (I remember a tropical house in the

A greenhouse allows you to grow tropical plants like these bromeliads in less than tropical climates.

An aluminium-framed greenhouse, where the owner has elected to make planting beds (instead of shelves to hold pots) on either side of the central path, so as to have fresh tomatoes in winter.

Royal Botanic Gardens in Sydney where there were beds carpeted in AFRICAN VIOLETS under the benches.) The full-height glass also allows you the option of omitting the bench and planting directly in the ground; there's no need to put in a floor except for a path down the middle, and an earth floor helps to keep the humidity up, something most greenhouse plants enjoy. Normally the foundations are simply baulks of treated timber which you lay on a bed of sand, but concrete is more durable, if more difficult for the do-it-yourselfer.

TIMBER OR ALUMINIUM?

If you decide to go for a custom design, then you'll probably be framing your greenhouse in timber. This won't allow quite so much light as the finer aluminium trusses do, but the difference is small, and timber is easier to build with and allows you to screw in cup hooks for hanging baskets and what have you. Western red cedar is first choice, as lesser woods rot easily in the damp heat and painting them is a chore, but treated pine is satisfactory and a good deal cheaper. You needn't clad your structure in glass; clear plexiglass is just as good and less liable to be smashed in hailstorms; clear corrugated fibreglass isn't pretty, but it

will serve. You can even clad the whole thing in heavy polythene for economy's sake: a great many commercial greenhouses in Europe and the United States use it, but it needs replacing every three years or so as it deteriorates in the sunlight. As long as the roof doesn't leak — one of the pleasures of a greenhouse is being able to garden when it's raining outside — it won't matter if the walls aren't quite watertight. And if they're not airtight it doesn't matter either — the problem is almost always insufficient ventilation rather than too much — unless you really are trying to maintain tropical temperatures when there's frost outside.

LOOKING AFTER IT

Looking after a greenhouse is simple enough. You give the plants the usual attention they like in the way of water, fertiliser and repotting, and keep the temperatures in the range they like. A thermometer hanging somewhere in the middle of the house is a great help. The routine is simple. In winter, close the ventilators at night, then open them a little in the morning unless the weather really is cold. In summer, the problem is to keep the house from getting too hot: most plants languish above about 30°C, and it's quite easy for an unshaded greenhouse to heat up to 50°C or more. Put SHADECLOTH over the roof during the spring, and keep your ventilators, and maybe the door, open wide. You can automate your watering, using the same sort of small sprinklers that you use in the garden, but if you are growing a wide range of plants you may prefer to water them

individually by hand. Hosing everything down with a fine spray from time to time will keep the humidity buoyant (the air dries out as the temperature goes up) and discourage red spider, the main greenhouse pest. Bugs can run rampant in the humid warmth, so occasionally you'll have to spray. The easiest way to do it is to buy a greenhouse smoke bomb, close all the ventilators, set it off and then retreat until the air has cleared again. And it's a good idea to empty all the plants out into a shady spot once every summer and give the house a thorough cleaning and overhaul, painting and replacing putty in the windows, oiling the ventilator hinges and so on, as needed. Not that most of us actually do it; we prefer to just enjoy our plants.

A greenhouse doesn't have to be big or glamorous! Some wonderful orchids grow in this simple structure, whose frame was improvised from the slats of a discarded futon-bed, its sides clad with polythene sheeting and its roof with corrugated fibreglass. With shelves and stands in place to hold all the pots, there is just enough room inside to turn around.

For many people, the great allure of having a greenhouse is being able to grow the more delicate orchids, like the beautiful Cattleya trianaei from Colombia.

HERBS

To a botanist, a herb is any plant without permanent woody stems — anything, that is, that is not a tree or a shrub — but gardeners call 'herbs' those plants that we grow to add savour to our cooking, never mind that rosemary, for example, is a shrub or the bay tree a tree.

While most of our herbs will put up with poor soil and drought, they shouldn't have to: they flourish best in good soil and with the same watering that the rest of the garden gets. And almost without exception they like sunshine.

No need to grow them in special herb gardens, modelled on those of medieval monasteries or otherwise; they will be perfectly happy to bring their fragrance and softly coloured foliage (few can be described as outstanding in flower) anywhere you fancy them. Try parsley or sage as an edging to set off brilliant flowers, or one of the lower-growing lavenders to mask the bad legs of roses or chrysanthemums; add the bold leaves and flower heads of angelica to a herbaceous border; or just place some eau de cologne mint next to a path where you can brush past it and release its delicious perfume.

HILLS, HILLING

When you are told to plant your pumpkin seeds or strawberry crowns on 'hills', it doesn't mean that you should move to the mountains. A 'hill' just means a mound of soil, maybe 15 or 20 centimetres high and three times as wide. The idea is to ensure that the crown of the plant will never get damp and thus be prey to fungus, and the fruit won't be dragging in the mud. If your soil is well drained, there is no need to go to the trouble. 'Hilling' or 'hilling up' means heaping soil around

The traditional formal herb garden in miniature, making a pleasant and fragrant incident on a large, brick-paved patio. There is no need to have one type to a bed; mixing-and-matching, as here, allows the cook more variety.

the base of a plant, either to protect it from extreme cold or to blanch its stems for the kitchen, and is the same as EARTHING UP.

HONEY FUNGUS

A major problem in Britain, but fortunately less common in Australia, *Armillaria mellea* is a disaster when it invades a garden. It usually starts life on the underground parts of tree stumps or other rotting wood, but can then run through the ground to infest the roots of living trees and shrubs, killing them. No species is known to be immune, and once the tree starts to die it is usually too late. If, on digging up some roots, they appear to be tied up with bootlaces and have the characteristic faint honey odour, there is nothing for it but to remove the tree, roots and all, and burn it. There are chemicals with which the soil can be drenched to kill the fungus, but they are very poisonous and are best applied by a professional.

If you are clearing trees or shrubby undergrowth, it is a wise precaution to grub out the stumps with as much root as possible.

HORMONES

Like all living things, plants produce hormones, in minute quantities, which regulate their growth and metabolism. Artificial hormones form the active ingredients of some weedkillers, and also of preparations designed to assist cuttings to make roots. Just dip the end of the cutting in the powder or solution before you plant it — but make sure the stuff is fresh. Rooting hormone has a fairly short shelf life, and if it has been sitting around in the shop or your shed it may have lost its potency. You can try brushing a little on the bare roots of roses, fruit trees or orchids at planting time too.

HOW BIG?

Any decent book on plants will tell you how tall a particular plant will grow, though its spread, which you also need to know if you are to SPACE your

plantings properly, is often left out, leaving you to apply the (very vague) rule of thumb that most plants grow about two-thirds as wide as tall. But bare dimensions are abstract things, difficult for even the experienced to visualise. Architects — good ones anyway — have long been accustomed to measuring dimensions against the human body, and gardeners can do so too.

HYDROPONICS

The art of growing plants without soil, their roots being kept in a tank of dilute nutrient solution, which may be filled with sand or perlite to hold the plants up; alternatively they can have their crowns supported by some sort of horizontal trellis laid over the tank. Commercial growers of carnations, tomatoes and indoor plants sometimes use the technique, which allows very precise control of the plants' hygiene and diet, and saves having to renew the soul in their greenhouses for successive crops. But the closest most of us ever come to practising hydroponics is rooting cuttings of things like *Coleus* or *Impatiens* in a glass of water.

Hydroponics at its most basic — a hyacinth growing in a hyacinth vase of water, its young shoot kept in the dark by a foil hat until flower buds appear.

Out of season

Ever since the days of the ancient Romans, people with pretensions to enjoying the simple life have poked fun at gardeners' fondness for persuading plants to perform outside their natural season, but it's still fun to do, and not at all difficult.

It isn't always possible to imitate the methods of the market growers; chrysanthemums, for instance, naturally bloom as the days get shorter in the autumn, and the cut blooms and potted chryssies you find at other times of the year have been grown in greenhouses that are blacked out with heavy curtains for a few hours each day to fool the plants into thinking that autumn is on its way. Simple enough in theory, but unless you have a greenhouse that you can devote entirely to out-of-season chrysanthemums it's easier just to buy them if the mood strikes you.

Sometimes we extend the natural season as a matter of course, as when we make staggered plantings of gladiolus

A pot of tulips like this is a joy at any time, but even more so in mid-winter. They are treated the same way as daffodils.

corms or peas, so that the later plantings will come on when the earlier ones are over. If we choose an early-maturing variety for our first plantings and a late one for the subsequent ones, we get another few weeks of flowers or peas, but most of us wouldn't think of these as being 'out of season'.

For most of us, a rosebush covered in bloom in mid-winter would be, but in our generally mild-wintered climates that isn't at all difficult to arrange. It's just a matter of choosing an amenable variety like 'Lorraine Lee', the climber 'Nancy Hayward' or one of the old Tea Roses like 'General Gallieni', planting it in a warm sunny spot, and giving it a light trim and some fertiliser in mid-autumn so that it will have buds on the way before the cold weather sets in — and *voila!* winter roses!

POTTING BULBS

1 *First, give the bulbs (these are daffodils) six weeks or so of artificial winter in the vegetable drawer of the refrigerator. Then put ordinary potting mix in an attactive flower pot.*

2 *For the most generous display, cram the pot with as many bulbs as it will hold, as long as you don't have to crush them to fit them into the pot.*

3 *The noses of the bulbs should just peek out at soil level. water the pot, and then put it in a cool, dark place. A cupboard in the shed will suit, or you might like to bury the whole thing in a shaded spot in the garden.*

If you have a greenhouse, or even a sunny kitchen window, you can have very early tomatoes by sowing them in the warmth in mid-winter and either keeping them inside or planting them out when the spring warms up; or you could sow them in autumn in pots, bringing them under glass when cold weather threatens, to have fresh tomatoes for the winter

Chrysanthemums flower as the days get shorter; nurseries fake this by drawing blackout curtains in their greenhouses for several hours a day. If you have a suitable spot indoors, or in a cold frame, you might like to try it, beginning to draw your curtains when the plants have made plenty of growth.

4 *When the shoots are well advanced and you can see the flower buds emerging among the leaves, bring the pot into a well lit room, and in a fortnight or so you will have a display like this, at least a month before the daffodils bloom in the garden. In a cool room the flowers should last three weeks. After bloom, plant them out in the garden.*

FORCING

It's usually easier to bring on a plant earlier than normal (to **force** it) rather than to delay its flowering, and the easiest (and most spectacular) are hyacinths, which you can arrange to have in flower in mid-winter. You simply give the bulbs an artificial winter by putting them in the vegetable tray of the refrigerator for a couple of months, and pot them up in late autumn, keeping them in a cool dark place (I put them in a dark cupboard in the shed), bringing them into the warmth and light of the house as soon as the flower buds make their appearance in the middle of the shoot, when they will bloom in about ten days. Daffodils, Dutch irises, tulips and anemones respond well to the same treatment, and so do hippeastrums (amaryllis) and freesias, but these last are tender, and you will have to turn the refrigerator as warm as it will go, and give them only a month or so of chilling.

Spring blossoms like flowering peaches, cherries, *Chaenomeles japonica*, forsythia and lilac can be forced too. They are even easier: just cut flowering branches as soon as the buds show signs of movement and bring them inside to open, treating them like any cut flower. They will be at least a fortnight earlier than in the garden, but they will lose colour, lilac often becoming quite white. Never mind; the pastel tones they assume are quite lovely. Alternatively, you can grow them in pots and bring the whole plant inside, placing it in a sunny window. Extend the repertoire with such things as viburnum, wisteria (which flowers very well as a pot plant but doesn't last when cut) and Japanese maples, for the freshness of their young leaves. Mist them occasionally for humidity, and put them back outside as soon as the flowers are over.

USING A GREENHOUSE

If you have a greenhouse, your scope is greatly extended. You can bring all sorts of things into winter bloom simply by planting them in pots and bringing them into the warm greenhouse as the weather cools off in autumn. The routine for roses is typical. Pot your roses (into 25 centimetre pots) in the normal winter season, grow them in the garden through the summer, and then bring them into the greenhouse about the end of March, trimming them back a bit, spraying in case they bring in bugs, and giving them some fertiliser to encourage the shoots that will bear the winter blooms. Give them plenty of light, and keep the spray gun handy, as mildew flourishes in the greenhouse. You won't be able to give them their regular pruning; just cut the blooms with long stems to keep the bushes compact. In the spring, they can go back out into the garden as the greenhouse will be too hot for them in summer. Try perpetual flowering carnations, gerberas, anemones, November lilies (*Lilium longiflorum*), tomatoes, strawberries and violets also. They are a little simpler — just pot them up in autumn and put them in the greenhouse.

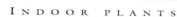

INDOOR PLANTS

Although the inside of a house away from the fresh air, rain and sunshine is for a plant what a diplomat would call a hardship posting, it's surprising what you can grow indoors. If you have a modern house where the sun can stream in through vast windows, you can bring in all sorts of things that we normally grow outside — fuchsias, azaleas, camellias, even hibiscus. But most of us are confined by smaller windows (and the desire to keep our curtains closed for privacy) to the standard favourites: palms, philodendrons and the like — and aspidistras where nothing else is able to survive.

Whatever you choose, the three golden rules are enough light, enough humidity, and no overwatering — more indoor plants drown than die of drought. It always seems that the spot in the room where a plant would do most for the decor is the darkest; after all, we like to put our furniture where we can sit in the light ourselves. If you can't rearrange to bring the plant nearer the window, you might like to have two (or even three) and rotate them so that each one has to spend only a week or two inside while its mate is recovering in a sunroom or a sheltered spot outdoors. Generally, flowering plants and those with variegated leaves need more light than plain green, non-blooming ones, but unnaturally dark leaves and lank, etiolated growth as the plant reaches for the light are always warning signs. Dust on the leaves robs a surprising amount of light. If you can't put your plants out in the warm rain every so often, they will need an occasional wipe over with a damp cloth. I wouldn't bother with 'leaf shine' preparations: they aren't cheap, and many plants dislike them.

It's hard to describe the peculiar, listless look of a plant that is suffering from too-dry air; it won't actually wilt, but it looks as though it wants to. Especially if air-conditioning or central heating has dried the air to a Sahara-like state, you might want to invest in a room humidifier. Failing that, you can spray the foliage with water every few days, but that won't do the wallpaper or the carpet much good; a better idea is to stand the pot on a tray of pebbles, over which you pour a little warm water occasionally, to give the plant a Turkish bath. It's much easier to keep the humidity up to a cluster of plants than to only one. Or you can confine your indoor gardening to the steamier air of the bathroom, and have the Tarzanish pleasure of showering amid greenery. (But keep hot water and soap off the plants.) Kitchens are usually humid, and well lit too, but beware of the fumes from gas stoves, which are very bad for plants, as are gas living-room heaters.

The ideal room for indoor plants, with plenty of light. Here you could grow almost anything, from orchids to palm trees, but the owner (or her decorator!) has opted for hanging baskets of ferns.

Just because the surface soil in the pot is dry doesn't mean the plant is thirsty. The standard test is to tap the side of the pot: if you get a dull thud, the soil is still moist; a clear sound indicates it's dry. But this works much better with old-fashioned terracotta than with plastic. If you can't resist frequent watering, at least don't leave your plants sitting in saucers full of water.

'Self-watering' pots are a boon to the erratic gardener: they are designed so that the plant takes what water it needs from a reservoir in the bottom. Most plants flourish in them, but you must use clean water, preferably rainwater, or there will be a build-up of salts in the soil, which the plant will *not* like.

Every so often, your plant will appreciate a little fertiliser. Slow release formulations like 'Osmocote' are the best, even if they are expensive. Go lightly; it's easy to over-fertilise. BLOOD AND BONE or dilute MANURE WATER would be marvellous too, except that they will stink the house out. Should pests like mealy bugs or red spider strike (they shouldn't if the air is humid enough), they will need to be dealt with. Swabbing them a couple of times with methylated spirits should do the trick: it is the height of foolishness to spray toxic insecticides indoors.

INFLORESCENCE

A useful bit of botanese this: it means the part of the plant immediately concerned with carrying the flowers, which may be arranged in a number of basic ways. Thus we have the **spike** of a gladiolus or of wheat, the **raceme** of a delphinium or foxglove, the **panicle** of lilac or a bunch of grapes, the **umbel** seen in agapanthus and (on a much smaller scale) in most eucalypts, the **corymb** of a hydrangea and so on. Of course, in common talk, we refer to flowers as being carried in sprays or clusters too, and rose fanciers are fond of the term 'truss', the inflorescence of the rose not really fitting neatly into the usual classifications.

INSECTICIDES

An insecticide can do its dirty work in one of three ways: it can kill the insect on **contact**; it might coat the plant's leaves so that the insect munches a dose of poison with its lunch (and is then called a **stomach poison**); or it might enter the plant's sap (**systemic** insecticides), making it poisonous to its enemies — and to people too. The length of time an insecticide remains effective (its **residual action**) varies; the systemics, which don't get washed off by the next shower, last the longest. Unfortunately, the longer-lasting insecticides also tend to be the most toxic; happily, the chemical companies are finally beginning to develop less toxic insecticides and the dangerously poisonous and polluting chlorinated hydrocarbons, like Lindane, Dieldrin and Parathion, are rarely seen now.

In the technology-happy fifties, gardeners were exhorted to get out the spray gun and squirt dangerously toxic chemicals everywhere the minute a bug appeared, but now that we are alert to the dangers of such behaviour, most people prefer to use as few poisons as possible. Especially, of course, on plants that we are planning to eat. Often a strong jet from the hose will dislodge and drown bugs like APHIDS and red spider mites (which hate a bath), and things like CATERPILLARS can be simply squashed. But every so often we are

faced with a plague that simply has to be sprayed. The rule is to use the smallest amount of the least toxic chemical possible, and if you have to spray a plant you are planning to eat, to scrupulously observe what is called the **with-holding period,** the time after which the insecticide will have dissipated sufficiently for safety. (Normally the package will say something like 'do not spray less than X weeks before harvest'.)

Old-fashioned TOBACCO WATER will kill many a bug, and so will the commercial preparations based on pyrethrum (Clensel is a well-known one). Recently, synthetic pyrethroids like 'Mavrik' have been introduced, which the makers claim are highly effective and not in the least dangerous, but such claims have been made before, and it is still wise to treat all insecticides as dangerous poisons. See CHEMICALS: USING THEM WISELY and the feature SAFETY IN THE GARDEN.

INSECT PESTS

Don't run off shrieking for the spray gun at the first sight of a bug — not all insects are pests. Check first that it is actually eating your plant, and then that it has appeared in sufficient numbers to do real damage. Insects are a fact of gardening life, and a few blemishes on your plants aren't likely to

Red spider is so tiny all the naked eye usually sees is the damage.

Lacebug, a common pest of azaleas, most invasive in dry weather.

be the end of the world.

Insects eat either by sucking the sap, as APHIDS and SCALE INSECTS do, or by chewing bits off, as is the habit of CATERPILLARS, beetles and most other bugs. Sucking insects are easily killed by contact INSECTICIDES; to do in the others, you have to coat the plant with poison, which they take in with their lunch. The number of insect pests is legion, but fortunately most have only one or two particular favourite plants; listing them all would call for a book on its own. Often you can catch the insect at work, but if you can't (many are decidedly fly-by-night creatures), take a sample of the damage down to your local nursery to identify the culprit and how to deal with it.

INSECTS, BENEFICIAL

By no means all insects are the gardener's enemies. Many do good: like bees, which pollinate flowers; ladybirds and lacewings, which eat aphids; and mantises, which eat quite a variety of harmful insects. And of course butterflies, as well as pollinating, are a delight to watch, even if their CATERPILLARS sometimes do make nuisances of themselves. Make sure that an insect is actually eating your plants before you resolve to destroy it.

INVASIVE PLANTS

Like Third World dictators, some plants will try to take over as much territory as they can — by making runners (like mint), layering branches where they touch the ground (like boysenberries or raspberries), or producing vast quantities of offsets (like montbretias), or seeds (like forget-me-nots). If a plant is described as invasive, it's a warning to consider whether it will give sufficient return in beauty, fragrance, fruit or whatever for the work of keeping it in bounds. You may, of course, decide to give such a plant its head, maybe to cover a rough spot, and

Vinca major is a bit too invasive to be allowed in mixed company, but on its own it is a first-rate groundcover.

one person's 'invasive thug' is another's 'easy-going, willing performer'. Invasiveness, like beauty, can be in the eye of the beholder.

Of course, weeds are invasive, by definition, but no one ever actually plants them.

IRON

One of the more important of the TRACE ELEMENTS, iron gets chemically bound up and inaccessible to plants in strongly ALKALINE soil. If this happens, there will be distinct symptoms of CHLOROSIS and stunted growth. It is no use just burying a few rusty nails, because the iron will rapidly get bound up, and relief will be temporary. The answer is to use an expensive chemical called **iron chelates** (or chelated iron; 'Sequestrine' is a well-known brand), and to take what steps you can to make the soil more acid (see ACID and ALKALINE). It is better to sidestep the problem altogether by growing any lime-hating plants in containers of acid potting mix if your garden soil is alkaline.

Excessive lime in the soil is almost certainly the cause of these lemon tree leaves turning yellow (CHLOROSIS). Iron chelates should restore their healthy green.

JARGON

Ask a botanist to explain the difference between a hippeastrum, the gorgeous (and expensive) 'Amaryllis' often grown as a pot plant, and the similar but much daintier, summer-flowering much-flowering Scarborough lily (*Vallota speciosa*), and you will be told something like, 'In *Vallota* the filaments of the anthers are partially adnate to the segments of the perianth, and in *Hippeastrum* they are not.' (Translation: the stamens of the *Vallota* are joined to the petals for about half their length, whereas those of a *Hippeastrum* are, as it were, completely freestanding in the centre of the flower.) And there are gardeners who adore botanese like this.

That is not to say that the jargon that gardening has borrowed from botany (and forestry too)is always pretentious and opaque (what would we do without words like annual and perennial, let alone such common terms as tree or shrub), nor that gardening doesn't have its own language. Just about all human activities do, and that of gardening is perhaps more familiar than most: management consultants have been heard to refer to 'pruning out the dead wood', and churchmen to decry places they see as 'hothouses' of vice.

But it is still easy to lapse into gardenese; I remember having to explain to a mystified editor that a 'grass joint' was not something one smoked but a space between paving stones, filled not with cement but earth where grass could grow.

▲ A hippeastrum in full glory, its flowers the size of saucers. It is native to South America; its cousin the Scarborough lily comes from South Africa.

▼ Look closely at this vallota, and you can see how the stamens are attached to the petals for about half their length. But to the gardener the main difference is that it is only half as big as the hippeastrum, and flowers two months later.

You can't garden without tools

The tools of the gardener have changed surprisingly little over many centuries: archaeologists have found spades and hoes used by the Ancient Romans that could pass for modern ones, and the Chinese were making iron hoes at the same time. Just about the only modern innovation has been the lawnmower, which arrived at the end of the eighteenth century, but didn't get power until very recently. In the old days the lawn was mown by a gang of men with scythes and was thus a rich man's luxury.

THE ESSENTIAL TOOL KIT

One result of all this history is that there are surprisingly few tools that you really need to garden successfully. Our ancestors weren't as fond of gadgets as we are, and they developed multi-purpose implements. Apart from the **lawnmower** (and in a small garden you might, by clever design, dispense with both the lawn and machine), the basic kit is: a **spade** for big digging, a **trowel** for small cultivation, for weeding and for planting things; a pair of **secateurs** for small pruning (like roses) and cutting flowers; a **pruning saw** for heavier pruning; a **wheelbarrow**; and a **rake** (which can do double duty in preparing seed beds) and a **broom** for cleaning up. To these you should add a good pair of **gardening gloves**. Some people don't like them, but you soon get used to the feel, and they do keep your hands clean and protected from scratches and broken fingernails. Buy two pairs: like socks, one of the pair has a habit of hiding when you're looking for them. You'll need a **hose**, of course, with at least one **sprinkler** and a **rose attachment** for hand watering. The attachments that simply allow you to snap these on and off, and to snap the hose onto the tap, are a great innovation. They are usually made of plastic, which doesn't last all that long if you leave them out in the sun, but they aren't expensive to replace every few years.

It is often possible to improvise if a specialised tool isn't available. Bonsai enthusiasts, for instance, are apt to find regular secateurs or trowels too cumbersome and make much use of such things as nail scissors, tweezers, kitchen knives and forks, even chopsticks.

SUPPLEMENTARY TOOLS

If you have a lawn, a small pair of **edging shears** will be called for. The best are the old-fashioned hand shears that used, long ago, to be used for shearing sheep, but they aren't easy to find these days. Some people swear by a gadget that cuts the edge with a flailing piece of fishing line. Then you might add a **large (border) fork** for cultivating beds and lifting bulbs and potatoes; a **small hand fork** to match the trowel; and a pair of **long-handled loppers** for pruning those branches too big for the secateurs but too small to really need the saw; and a pair of **hedge shears** if you fancy clipped hedges and topiary. My grandfather, a farmer, swore by his **mattock** for digging out big weeds and preparing his vegetable beds, and his **hoe** for weeding, but I never use either.

Most insecticides and fungicides can be bought in aerosol cans, but if you are planning to grow fruit, roses, gladioli or other things that need regular medicine, a **spray gun** is desirable. Brass hand guns are expensive and tiring to use, and the chemicals are apt to corrode their rubber washers. Mechanically operated guns are really only worth the trouble if you are tending an orchard, and for years I've made do with a small gadget that couples to the end of the hose; it wasn't expensive, and it's easy to clean. Buy two, one for weedkillers and one for medicine, and mark each prominently to guard against confusion and disaster.

And that's it! You're now set to tackle the largest garden.

Everything else, from electrically powered hedge clippers to flame-guns for weeding to revolving compost bins to electric edge-trimmers and the mechanical monsters that chew prunings into little chips to make mulch — and the manufacturers of such things come up with more all the time — is gadgetry that you can indulge in if you are so inclined. Ask to see a demonstration of gadgets like these, before you decide they might be useful.

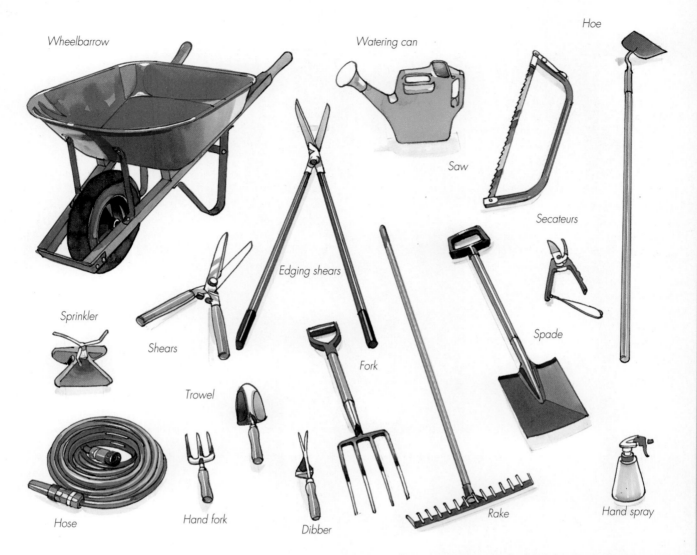

Wheelbarrow

Watering can

Hoe

Saw

Secateurs

Edging shears

Sprinkler

Shears

Spade

Trowel

Fork

Hose

Hand fork

Dibber

Rake

Hand spray

BUYING TOOLS

Choose the best quality tools you can afford, and they should last long enough to leave to your grandchildren. Most come in several sizes, and while it's unwise to buy tools too small for the job, it's equally so to buy something you find cumbersome: go through the motions of using them in the shop to see how they suit. It may seem a trivial point, but if you can choose brightly coloured handles, they'll be easier to find when you put them down in the garden. Wooden handles can always be painted yellow or orange, but plastic rarely takes paint easily. One could wish that the makers of secateurs, particularly, would think of this and not make them in discreet camouflage colours. Lawnmowers are discussed in the feature LAWNS WITHOUT TEARS.

CARING FOR TOOLS

It may sound obvious enough, but put them away when you've finished with them! Tools aren't meant to endure the weather, and few things are more frustrating than to search high and low for the secateurs, to cut a bunch of roses for one's favourite aunt, only to find them lying rusty among the zinnias where you were using them last week. Keep them secure, not only to guard against accidents, but because burglars find things like trowels useful for forcing windows open. If you keep the tools in a shed, lock it! Spades, forks and saws can be hung on cup hooks on the shed wall, smaller tools placed on a shelf or in a box (an old milk crate will do). Tools get both wet and dirty in use; wipe the dirt off with a damp rag, and wipe over with an oily one occasionally. A drop of oil in the hinges of secateurs and shears is a great help too. Blades need a swipe with a sharpening stone sometimes; you don't really need a keen edge on a spade, but it should be sharp enough to cut rather than tear any roots it might encounter. Secateurs are finicky to sharpen unless you disassemble them. I tried once and couldn't work out how to get them back again properly; their replacements go to a knife sharpener once a year. Send the saw along with them, unless you're sure you can do the job yourself without bloodshed.

If you break the wooden handle of a spade or fork, you can replace it; most of the large hardware suppliers can do it for you. But if you're in the habit of breaking things, you're using the wrong tool for the job.

JASMINE

Here is a good example of the desirability of taking the trouble to master botanical names, for the name 'jasmine' has been applied at various times to almost any twining plant with scented flowers, and to quite a few shrubs too. Thus we have the Carolina jasmine or jessamine (*Gelsemium sempervirens*), the cape jasmine (*Gardenia jasminoides*), the night-scented jasmine (*Cestrum nocturnum*), the confederate or star jasmine (*Trachelospermum jasminoides*), the Chilean jasmine (*Mandevillea laxa*) — none of which is related to the 'true' jasmine (*Jasminum*) or even to each other.

You might prefer the all-year sprinkling of flowers of *Jasminum azoricum* to the (admittedly gorgeous) ten-day display of the scruffy and INVASIVE *J. polyanthum* — or the year-round handsomeness and versatility of the star jasmine, equally good as a climber or groundcover, to either.

The star jasmine, with its evergreen leaves and early-summer flowers, their scent stronger and sharper than those of any other jasmine.

Jasminum azoricum, a rather shrubby climber, with glossy dark leaves.

Jasminum polyanthum is sometimes called the pink jasmine, but only the unopened buds are pink.

K

The chemist's symbol for POTASSIUM, most often encountered in the formulation NPK on fertiliser packages.

KIKUYU

Pennisetum clandestinum, a kind of creeping millet from East Africa, and a valuable evergreen pasture grass, is happiest where it gets summer rain and little frost. If you're thinking of planting a lawn with it, make yourself comfortable; pour yourself a drink if you like. Now, close your eyes and picture yourself mowing (and trimming edges) twice as often as you would with a fine grass like couch or bent, and fighting endless war with the wildly invasive kikuyu as it sends metres-long runners into every planting bed within reach, strangling everything in its way. Sanity will soon return. See the special feature LAWNS WITHOUT TEARS for some better alternatives.

Unmown for three weeks, kikuyu is well on the way to reducing this garden to a jungle.

KITCHEN GARDEN

Time was when vegetables and fruit trees were grown somewhere down at the bottom of the garden, as though they weren't quite fit to be seen until they had been harvested and the cook had had her way with them. But if you take pride in bringing your produce to the table, why not give your kitchen garden a place of honour in your garden design? Neat rows of vegetables have a beauty of their own, in part the elegance of good horticultural craftsmanship, in part the anticipation of delights to come. You might try, for instance, cutting a formal pattern of simple beds on the lawn, like an old-fashioned rose garden, with neat edging plantings of things like parsley or strawberries; making the paths between your blocks of plantings in a permanent material like brick rather than just soil; or planting a BORDER with a mix of vegetables, fruit and herbs rather than with merely ornamental plants — and of course, you can always add some flowers (to cut for the house) if you find the greens and greys of the edible plants too subtle.

However you design it, let your kitchen garden be in the sun, but out of the wind, and on the very best soil you have. But it is likely you'll still want to place it in the back garden where it is safe from light-fingered passers-by and romping dogs.

The trouble with a kitchen garden is the gaps that appear when you harvest. This one solves that by a formal plan, with brick paths and edgings of clipped box — even when the beds are stripped bare, there is still pattern to delight the eye. (Rosemary could replace the box if you want everything to be edible.)

Lawns without tears

Every time you hear someone say 'I hate gardening', you can bet that close behind will be 'especially mowing the lawn!' Lawn work is like housework — mostly only noticed when it isn't done. Never mind that grass is soft and quiet underfoot, comfortable for children (and grown-ups) to play on, and doesn't reflect heat and glare — a shaded lawn is cooler than even the best shaded patio in the summer — we all like the idea of a lawn that takes as little work as possible, even those perfectionists among us who won't be content with anything other than a perfect, velvet-like sward.

START WITH CAREFUL DESIGN

Whether you're making a new lawn or are dealing with an established one, take a critical look at its layout. Is it (or will it be) simply too big? Could you introduce more paving (most patios are too small anyway) or extend your planting areas with shrubs or GROUNDCOVERS which, being low growing, won't make the garden seem smaller, even if you can't walk on most of them? Could its design be simplified to eliminate fussy flower beds and tight corners where it's difficult to manoeuvre the mower? Could you extend nearby planted areas into the shady spots under trees where grass tends to be patchy? Might groundcovers be appropriate here, or could you naturalise BULBS like bluebells or freesias in the grass for a spring display — and an excuse not to mow until their foliage has died down? Should banks where mowing is awkward and possibly dangerous (any with a slope steeper than about one in three) be planted with groundcovers? Will the lawn be edged with paving or with massed shrubs (under whose overhang you can tuck the mower) to eliminate trimming edges as much as possible? Do you have uncomfortable changes of level at the edges of your beds, with rows of rocks to bang the mower against, or the sort of gutter beloved of municipal gardeners? If you keep your beds and the grass at the same level, you can even indulge

Couch (Cynodon dactylon) is Australia's favourite lawn grass, flourishing in our warm climate. It likes sun, and it is worth mixing it with the more shade-tolerant bent, which will form the dominant grass where the lawn spreads into the shade of trees. The bent will also keep the lawn lush in winter when the couch tends to go dormant.

Kentucky bluegrass (Poa pratensis) is perhaps the choicest of all fine lawn grasses, happiest in a cool climate. It isn't blue at all, though it is a softer green than couch.

in allowing plants to spill over the edges to soften the line. With practice, you can get the mower quite close and minimise hand trimming; just don't use fragile things like lobelias or begonias which can't take the occasional bump.

And there is always the option of eliminating grass altogether, relying on paving (or gravel, as they do in Italy) to surface where you walk and on extensive plantings of trees and ground covers or softness and coolness. Admittedly, this is easier to do on a small scale, and grass is much cheaper to install than paving — and in a dry summer even the brownest lawn is less dusty.

WHICH GRASS?

Lawn connoisseurs debate the merits of the various grasses — fescue versus bent, Queensland blue couch versus ordinary couch, Kentucky bluegrass versus buffalo — with as much fervour as wine buffs compare grape varieties. Even if the different species didn't have their own preferences about soils and climates, there is simply no one perfect grass. The best lawns (like some of the best wines!) are a balanced blend of varieties, selected to grow mainly in warm or cool weather, in the sunny or shady areas. Let local knowledge be your guide, and choose a blend of seed recommended by your local nursery for your area. (If you decide to establish your lawn from turf, you'll be offered what the local turf nursery thinks is the best in any case.) But choose one recommended for lawns, which will be made up of finer (and probably more expensive) varieties, rather than one of the coarser blends suitable for playgrounds and football fields. These may be faster to establish, but the advantage is only a few weeks, and you'll pay for your impatience with more frequent mowing. Coarser grasses are apt to make the garden look smaller too, rather the way a boldly patterned wallpaper makes a room look smaller. At all costs, avoid mixes with the tufty and weedy perennial rye-grass — and shun the wildly invasive KIKUYU for the weed it is. The velvet brigade will probably decry the

Even a small lawn offers a place for children to play and for adults to sit on the grass or sunbathe. And since there aren't miles of edges to trim, you can allow plants like the lavender in the middle of the picture to sprawl onto the grass a bit to soften the lines — the fiddly job of trimming under them by hand won't add much to the overall work.

addition of a little bit of clover (about 4 or 5 per cent), but most of us will welcome it for its greenness and the nitrogen that its roots will add to the soil. 'O'Connor's Strawberry Clover' is the best.

PREPARE YOUR GROUND

Don't forget that your lawn is made of plants, and as with any planting, preparing the bed well is half the road to success. CULTIVATE it thoroughly. This is a mighty job with a spade, and if it's a big area you might prefer to hire a rotary cultivator (rotary hoe) either with or without a professional operator.

People often bring in topsoil, enough to make a layer about 10 centimetres deep, but it is really better to improve what you have. Grass roots are lazy and inclined to stay in the imported soil layer rather than go deep as they should. If you need to improve your drainage, now is the time to do it. Incorporating a little sand before you cultivate (say a layer 4 or 5 centimetres deep) will help heavy soils to make a good seed bed, but if you rake over the surface to level out any bumps and hollows and to break it up finely and get rid of any stones and clods that might be lying about, that should be enough. Then water the bed thoroughly to encourage the weeds to germinate, and, after three weeks or so, zap them with GLYPHOSATE so that you start as you mean to continue, with weed-free ground.

It is an old tradition to plant a cleaning crop of potatoes first, the idea being that their leaves shade out the weeds, and digging up the potatoes cultivates the soil. Or you could plant a GREEN MANURE crop of clover if you prefer, or if you want to hold off making the lawn until other garden construction is out of the way. Dig it in when you're ready for the grass.

INSTALLING THE GRASS

Planting the lawn can be done in one of three ways: by sowing seed, the cheapest; by planting runners or sprigs, the most laborious; or by laying turf, the easiest and fastest (you get 'instant lawn'), but also the most expensive. Even so, the extra cost may not be budget-breaking if the lawn is fairly small.

In our mild climate, you can sow **seed** just about all year, though it may take its time about coming up in winter. But try to avoid sowing in the hottest part of summer or you'll go crazy trying to keep it watered. Spring and autumn are usually ideal, with a nod to spring if you have the choice. The seed package will tell you how much to allow per square metre (usually about 2 to 2.5 grams, or 2 to 2.5 kilograms for 100 square metres). You may want to mark out the lawn area in sections of, say, 10 square metres as a guide to quantities. Drawing lines on the ground with the rake handle will do. Buy a little extra seed, both as insurance against waste in the sowing and to over-sow any patches that don't grow properly. And check the 'sow by' date on the package. It helps to get an even sowing if you bulk up the seed with an equal volume of dry sand, and if you divide your batch of seed in half, walking down the length of the lawn scattering the first half, and then across it with the second. Then *lightly* rake over to cover the seed, and water thoroughly with the finest spray your hose can manage. Until the new grass is about 3 centimetres tall, you'll need to keep the ground moist, which will mean daily watering in warm weather. Then you can reduce the frequency of your watering to encourage the roots to go deep, and by the time the grass is ready for its first trim, when it is about 5 or 6 centimetres tall (set the mower as high as it will go) you should only need to water about once a week unless it's really hot. Try not to walk on the new grass until it has its first clip; it might be wise to remind people with a temporary fence made from a few stakes and some string.

Turf is the easiest way to start a lawn. You just buy the turf and lay it on your ground (which should be as carefully prepared as for seed) like so much carpet, butting the turves together. Trim them to fit at the edges with a large pair of scissors, saving the trimmings to plug any gaps and odd corners. Then sprinkle on some fine topsoil, enough to cover the green, and water it into the grass thoroughly. You can walk on it at once, but keep it moist at least for the first couple of weeks while it is making its roots, and go very gently on the first couple of mowings. Turf won't keep rolled up for more than a couple of days, so if you are planning to lay it on the weekend, order the delivery for as late in the week as possible, or plan on taking the day off if it arrives earlier. Most turf nurseries cut it pretty thin these days, but if you do get the odd one that's thicker than the others, you can shave its bottom with a large sharp knife.

You can, for economy, cut your turves with scissors or a sharp knife into sprigs about 2 centimetres square and plant these like any seedlings about 10 centimetres apart. They will grow together in a few weeks, but you'll need to keep a watch out for weeds establishing themselves between them. Or you can pull them apart completely into individual **runners**, planting these about 5 centimetres apart (they can

Trimming the edges can take as long as mowing, but it is just as important in keeping the lawn looking presentable. Timber, brick or concrete edgings on which one wheel of the mower can ride will all but eliminate the job, but it is difficult to make them inconspicuous enough to look 'natural'.

In a very small garden, you might consider the option of paving instead of grass. More expensive initially, but less work in the long run; and in a shaded garden like this one, keeping the grass vigorous will be a battle anyway.

just be scattered and then covered over with a sprinkling of fine soil and watered in). These will need as much attention with the hose as seed does, and it's best to only do about 15 to 20 square metres at a time, lest the runners dry out. Again you have to watch for weeds. Both methods will allow you to use only about 25 per cent as much turf, but they are a lot of work and overall probably no less trouble than seeding. Again, you can give the lawn its first haircut when the grass is about 5 centimetres tall.

MOWING AND MOWERS

It can be a great temptation to the lazy (or those with better ways to spend a Saturday) to mow the lawn as close as the mower will go in the hope of mowing less frequently, but you should resist it — shaving too close weakens the grass and allow weeds to get in. Even the finest of grasses shouldn't be cut closer than 2 centimetres, and 2.5 is better, especially in hot weather when the grass is under enough stress without having to cope with being beheaded. And if drought forces you to leave the lawn unwatered, it will cope better if you leave it longer still, say 3 or even 4 centimetres. It's better to mow when the grass is dry; it cuts more easily and doesn't clog the blades and the catcher. Mow first, and then water!

An old-fashioned hand mower is adequate for a small lawn, and the exercise of pushing it will do you good, but it must be looked after carefully: wipe it and oil the joints every time you use it, or it will rust up and become impossible to move. Most people opt for a power mower, either the usual rotary type or a more expensive reel model, which is a mechanised hand mower and needs nearly as much care to keep it in trim. The reel is the one if you are a lawn fanatic; it doesn't flail the grass the way a rotary does, and it is the only way to achieve the striped effect (caused by the way it lays the grass as you walk up and down) that looks so glamorous in photographs of English lawns. But most of us will forgo this refinement for the greater ease of maintenance of a rotary mower and its ability to cope with rough grass. Either type can be fitted with a grass catcher, and you should use it, as it isn't desirable to leave the clippings, no matter how fine, on the lawn. They'll just sift down through the grass and mat down to make **thatch**, which not only makes the lawn spongy and uncomfortable to walk on, it can choke the grass. (You can get rid of thatch by dragging a fine-tined stiff rake through the grass, which is apt to leave the lawn looking as though it has had an encounter with a drunken hairdresser.)

Petrol-driven mowers are noisy and give you the trouble of storing the petrol safely (in the garage, in a proper jerry-can). Most are four-stroke models these days, which means you have to check the oil, but don't use super-grade petrol or you'll burn the motor out. Electric mowers are quieter, but don't buy one operated with a cable; it can be fatal to accidentally run over it. Rechargeable models are apt to have a limited range and are only really suitable for a small garden. Of course, you'll keep safety in mind when you have the machine out. (See the feature on safety in the garden).

The no-mow lawn is an attractive idea, and the best plant to create one with is dichondra or kidney weed. It has its disadvantages: it needs lots of water in summer, and you can't use selective weedkillers on it, so you have to weed by hand. This can be nearly as big a job as mowing, and you can't really delegate it to a teenage member of the family. It is a good idea to try dichondra out on a small area before you commit yourself to it.

WEEDS AND OTHER PESTS

Weeds like paspalum, summer grass and flatweed spoil the appearance of a lawn, and, by growing faster and taller than the grass, force you to mow more often to keep everything looking presentable. Keep your grass growing strongly enough to maintain a tight cover by watering, deeply and infrequently, by not cutting it too close, and by giving it a light dressing of lawn fertiliser in spring and after summer's heat (water it in at once, or it will scorch the grass), and weeds should have little chance of getting in. The odd one will, and you can either just cut it out with an old kitchen knife, or spot treat it with GLYPHOSATE and allow the grass to grow over the gap. (Municipal parks departments spray the lot, grass and all, with selective weedkillers, which kill broad-leaved plants but not grass, but the weedkillers are poisonous and are apt to cause havoc if the spray drifts onto choice plants. Avoid them if you can.) If you are faced with an old and weedy lawn, removing the weeds can be a lot of work, and if there is less than about 50 per cent of good grass, you might prefer to simply rotary-hoe the lot and start afresh.

If your grass is flourishing, it should also shake off pests and diseases. Lawn grubs can cause trouble, eating the roots and making dead patches; try digging under a suspect dead patch and see if you find the fat grub. Squash it, and then water the lawn with a strong insecticide. Wet weather can bring on fungi like dollar spot, in which the grass dies off in small, mouldy-looking patches. Water the lawn with a fungicide; the problem will go away and the grass will grow back when the rain clears up. Mushrooms are a fungus, but they live mainly on humus rather than living roots, and even if they sometimes interfere with the grass, most of us would rather have the pleasure of fresh mushrooms than try to get rid of them. (But beware of toadstools.)

On any soil heavier than sand, walking (to say nothing of allowing people to park their cars on the grass) will compact the soil over time, and the grass roots will have a hard time of it. Its worth aerating the lawn every spring. You can do this simply by pricking it all over with a border fork, but it's easier to hire an aerator, most of which operate on a spiked roller (like a large version of the cylinder of a music box) from the garden centre.

Don't allow the idea of having a perfect lawn to run away with your gardening time and energy. If you have trees, shrubs and flowers to look at, a less than immaculate lawn won't seem quite so important in the garden picture.

LAYERING

An easy means of vegetative propagation, whereby you bend a shoot down to the ground and bury part of it so that it will, given time, make roots there. Plants that make runners, such as strawberries and violets, are prime candidates, but any plant with shoots sufficiently flexible to bend to the ground can be layered. It is the time-honoured way to propagate

rhododendrons and carnations; climbing roses, too. Raspberries, blackberries and their ilk will often layer themselves without assistance (one way that the feral blackberry makes such a pest of itself, and why in gardens they are grown on trellises like climbing roses).

LEGUMES

The pea family is one of the largest in the vegetable kingdom, including not only the peas and beans of the kitchen garden, but also flowers like lupins, wisteria, the running postman (*Kennedya rubicunda*) and many trees. They all have the ability to draw NITROGEN directly from in the soil — not all by themselves, but by exploiting bacteria that live in nodules on their roots. This is called nitrogen fixation, and it means not only that legumes

The scarlet runner bean is a typical legume, with the distinctively shaped flowers of its family.

LAYERING

1 To make a layer, first bend a shoot down to the ground, stripping any leaves that will be buried. Making a nick in it to encourage the root, and wiping it with rooting HORMONE are optional.

2 Bury the bare part of the shoot. A sharp kink is a help to the rooting process, as long as you don't actually break the stem. A small stake, or a brick laid on top, will hold everything steady.

3 When new roots have formed, (which may take a while — rhododendrons can take a year or so), you can separate the new plant, and transplant it to its new home at leisure.

rarely need nitrogen given to them in the form of fertiliser, but also that as their leaves fall and decompose, they add nitrogen to the soil around them. They are the most valuable of plants for GREEN MANURE, but when you pull out a finished crop of something like peas, you always leave a few roots behind and their nodules will enrich the soil too. This makes them useful in crop rotations, as they are inclined to leave the soil a little better than they found it.

LIME

Lime adds calcium to the soil, but its main use to the gardener is to make the soil more ALKALINE, to raise the pH for plants that like it, like cabbages and their tribe. It comes in several forms: quicklime and slaked lime, which will burn the skin off your hands — let alone any plant they touch — and ground limestone, which has no sting and is much the best kind for the gardener. **Dolomite** is a kind of ground limestone containing magnesium as an extra. I usually choose it, just out of caution, though magnesium deficiency isn't usually much of a worry in most soils.

MANURE

The dung of animals is perhaps the most valuable fertiliser there is. True, it doesn't provide, weight for weight, the proportion of usable nutrients that

chemical fertilisers do, but they don't feed the micro-organisms on which the health of the soil, and ultimately your plants, depends. And they don't have the beneficial effect on the soil structure that manure and compost have. Fresh manure not only smells, but it is also too rich and 'hot', and it is liable to burn plants it touches. Manure is best heaped and allowed to rot (to compost) for a couple of weeks before it is used. Cover the heap with an old tarpaulin or a sheet of plastic, both to keep the rain from leaching nutrients out and to discourage flies. It is ready when the smell of ammonia fades, and you can either dig it in where you want it, or spread it as mulch, as you please.

The only manure to avoid is human manure, from fear of spreading disease, though the Chinese have collected and composted 'nightsoil' for centuries; otherwise you can use any type that might become available. The nutrient value of manures varies a bit, as you might expect from a natural product, but poultry manure is generally regarded as the most concentrated and 'hottest': it needs to be used almost as sparingly as an artificial fertiliser. Cow manure is pretty rich too; horse or stable manure tends to be a mix of urine and straw, with little actual dung; it needs composting. Pig manure is held to be the 'coldest', but we rarely see it in the garden centre in Australia. Don't be surprised to get a crop of weeds after spreading manure; weed seeds are rarely digested. They'll pull up quite easily.

MANURE WATER

Made by putting a bucketful of manure in a hessian bag and steeping it like a giant tea-bag for a couple of days in a garbage bin full of water, manure water is a wonderful pick-me-up for plants in need of some instant fertiliser, or for pot plants like orchids. Also called liquid manure, it is the old-fashioned equivalent of the chemical-based liquid fertilisers in use today, though unlike them it is applied to the soil rather than the foliage: you can use it full strength

or dilute it. Its smell is its only drawback, but this soon dissipates as the soil absorbs the liquid.

MILDEW

There are nearly as many species of the mildew fungus as there are plants it attacks. Almost all mildews go for the young shoots, which are often slightly shrivelled-looking before the tell-tale grey mildew itself appears. There are both 'powdery' and 'downy' mildews. Both can cripple the young shoots of such plants as crepe myrtles, roses, cabbages and grapes. They look rather alike, through powdery mildews are inclined to leave the plant looking as though it has been dusted with (rather dirty) flour, and downy shrivels the leaves, with the mildew itself being less obvious. The damage they cause, and the remedies, are much the same. The French winegrower's custom of planting a rosebush at the end of each row of vines is not as romantic as it looks: the rose is slightly more susceptible to the fungus, and serves as an early warning to the vigneron to get out his spray gun — the vegetable equivalent of the miner's canary. Before the advent of copper-based FUNGICIDES, the control was dusting or spraying the plants with sulphur, which in hot weather can do as much damage as the fungus. Mildew is apt to attack when days are warm and nights cool, in the spring and autumn, and it is worst in dry weather. It's well worth augmenting your spraying with a thorough watering. Which fungicide to use depends on both the plant and the type of mildew: 'Benlate' and 'Bavistin' are currently in favour, but seek advice from your local nursery.

MINT

Mint is exceptional among herbs in liking a damp spot, so is traditionally grown around the (almost always leaking) garden tap. In all its varieties (peppermint, spearmint, apple mint, eau-de-cologne and pennyroyal), it is very invasive, though the pretty variegated apple mint is quite well

A pebble mulch protects the soil but does not add nutrients.

The variegated pineapple mint, at once the most decorative and least invasive of the tribe.

With its dense growth and fragrant leaves, mint makes a good, if not quite prostrate, ground cover for a damp spot. It does tend to die back for the winter, however.

A mulch of volcanic scoria looks attractive in a rock garden.

behaved, and of good flavour. To keep mint from taking over, try planting it in a tub sunk into the ground almost to its rim; you can use the trick for other takeover merchants too. Or else just use it as a ground cover in a place where it can romp as it pleases. Not too much shade, though.

MULCH

A mulch is a sort of blanket laid over the soil to keep it cool in summer and warm in winter, to conserve moisture, and to smother weeds. You can use almost anything: gravel, crushed bricks, shredded newspaper, sawdust, tanbark, wood chips, fallen leaves (even gum leaves), COMPOST, grass clippings,

Compost is the best of all mulches.

straw, or old MANURE — but not BLACK PLASTIC, which suffocates the soil. Organic materials (all but the first two) have the benefit that they eventually rot and add humus and nutrients to the soil. Sawdust, wood chips and newspaper (which is inclined to blow around) tend to starve the soil of nitrogen until they are well rotted; a light sprinkling of sulphate of ammonia (say a third of the dose recommended on the packet) on top won't go amiss.

Fresh grass clippings should be spread only very thinly — not more than a centimetre or so deep at each spreading, or they will get awfully slimy as well as hot and do more harm than good. They are best put on the compost heap. Gravel only needs to be deep enough to cover the surface; it's a nuisance in a bed where you plan to cultivate. Compost and manure, provided it is well rotted and has lost its heat, can be put on as thickly as you please. Ten centimetres is not too deep, as long as the crowns of plants aren't smothered, but most of us don't have that luxury: we spread what we have over the area where we want it to go.

Established weeds will grow up through a mulch, so start with weed-free ground. And don't put mulch on dry soil; water first so that there will be moisture to conserve.

There is no need to be purist about a native garden. The perfect blend of mostly natives with some choice exotics seen here is not difficult to achieve. All planting design, after all, is based on the gardener's sense of what goes with what.

NATIVE PLANTS IN THE GARDEN

Patriotic gardeners everywhere are apt to value their native plants above all others — as well they might, for the plants that have evolved in a particular place can bestow a sense of rightness, of being at home in the land, that no others quite can. But often they are led into forgetting that any country is a big place and unthinkingly accept as 'native' a plant that might have its home a long way away. Thus we see the native frangipani (*Hymenosporum flavum*) pining for the Queensland rainforests in Adelaide's dusty streets; plants from the dry country of Western Australia cheek by jowl with those from Victoria's cool mountain gullies.

Or the gardener has got the idea that Australian plants need little care, which by and large is true, but has not realised that many are short lived (nature having little use for long-lived shrubs in a land of regular bushfires), and is dismayed when the garden needs major replanting after only ten years or so. It is a paradox that the beautiful plants of the oldest continent should be most beautiful in their youth.

Australian soils are notoriously deficient in PHOSPHORUS (which is why farmers have been such lavish users of superphosphate), and many native plants not only don't need it added in fertiliser, they are quite allergic to it. Give them artificial fertiliser with a very sparing hand, but most of them like compost.

There is, of course, no reason why

Cestrum nocturnum *is the most deliciously scented of all the night-scented flowers. Too delicious for some people, who find its scent heavy and cloying. It is happiest in a frost-free climate.*

you shouldn't blend native plants with foreign (exotic) ones to suit your own taste. Indeed, if you want to plant deciduous trees for summer shade and winter sun, you'll be obliged to make the mix, as there are no deciduous Australian trees to speak of.

NEWSPAPER

Getting rid of old newspapers can be a problem, but they can be recycled in the garden. Not into more paper, but into (admittedly fairly low-grade) fertiliser. If you are allowed an incinerator by the local council, they can be burned to provide ASH. If not, they can be composted: add some poultry manure to get the process going or it will take forever. Or they can be spread, wet, as a mulch, of two or three sheets, or about 1 centimetre of shreds. Either way, they are best shredded first; if you have a lot to deal with, a cheap office shredder might prove a good investment.

A newspaper mulch isn't exactly pretty, and the shreds of paper tend to blow about. Some compost, manure, or bark chips on top will deal with both problems. Used like this, the newspaper can be a help in eking out a compost supply to give a reasonable depth of mulch, in the same way that a frugal cook adds ordinary fish to lobster tails to make them go further.

NIGHT-SCENTED FLOWERS

Even if you don't spend most of your days at work so that the evening is the main time for enjoying the garden, flowers that waft their perfume by night can make a summer evening on the terrace even more pleasant (mosquitoes permitting), and you can place them so that the scent comes inside through open windows too.

Think of the night-scented jasmine, *Cestrum nocturnum,* a rather dowdy shrub by day, tender to frost, but smelling like a French perfumer's shop after sunset; of the climbing moonflower (*Calonyction aculeatum*), opening great white saucers at dusk,

(fast enough to see them), and disliking cold too, but easily grown as an annual from spring-sown seed; of the night-scented cacti like *Epiphyllum oxypetalum*, which time their flowers for the full moon; of night-scented stocks (*Matthiola bicornis*); and of the many flowers that, scented in the daytime, seem to gain strength in the evening — frangipani, roses and petunias for instance.

NITROGEN

An essential element in protein, and hence of all living things. Insufficient nitrogen causes a plant to be stunted in growth, with small, pale leaves and poor flowering and fruiting. A super-abundance can lead to luxuriant foliage, often at the expense of flowers — a condition to be encouraged in such crops as lettuces and lawns, which is why lawn fertilisers are very high in the element.

Plants can't make use of the abundant nitrogen in the air (except for LEGUMES); they must take it up after it has married with other elements in compounds, notably the nitrates and ammonia. If the soil is to be maintained in good health and the garden to give regular bounty, these need to be constantly replenished — from fertilisers such as sulphate of ammonia and decaying organic matter like manure and compost.

NPK

Followed by a trio of numbers, as NPK 7:6:7 for example, this symbol on a fertiliser packet tells you the percentage by weight of NITROGEN (N), PHOSPHORUS (P), and POTASSIUM (K) the contents will make available to plants. (If all three are contained, it can be called 'complete fertiliser', but this need not mean that TRACE ELEMENTS are included too.) The proportions vary according to the intended purpose of the fertiliser: a lawn fertiliser will be high in nitrogen (say 9:4:6), one intended for shrubs, relatively higher in phosphorus and potassium (maybe 5:8:12).

It is possible to become fascinated by the NPK figures, and to clutter up the shed with half a dozen different fertiliser bags — one for the lawn, one for the camellias, one for the roses and so on — but in practice, it is easier to buy just one type, with the three fairly evenly balanced, say 7:6:7 or 8:8:8, and use it on everything. It is likely to be more economical too; blends different from a company's standard 'all purpose' one usually cost more.

All this refers to chemical fertilisers. Although it is possible to test organic fertilisers like manure and arrive at an NPK figure, they vary so much (being natural products) that it is rarely done. In any case, their benefits are far more than just the bare amounts of the big three elements they contain.

NUTGRASS

If they could talk, the papyrus of the ancient Egyptians and the water-chestnut of Chinese cookery would certainly disown their little brother *Cyperus rotundus*, officially the world's most troublesome weed. It grows almost everywhere. Don't let its innocent low tufts of grassy leaves fool you: its underground runners spread like wildfire, making a mat so tight that few plants can struggle through it. It's easy enough to dig up, but lurking in the soil are the pea-sized tubers (the 'nuts'), every one of which will start to grow at once if you miss it. Try digging nutgrass up when you see it, but keep some GLYPHOSATE handy to zap the inevitable regrowth. The poison works best in hot weather when the plant is dry, but even then you will probably need two or three applications; nutgrass is a lot tougher than it looks.

NUT TREES

Though there is a great Australian tradition of the backyard fruit tree, we don't often think to plant nut trees. Yet they are mostly easier to grow than fruit trees, needing no pruning and rarely any spraying. Consider almonds, happier in dry summer areas than their relatives the peaches, which they

The hanging chains of white flowers of the Queensland nut tree are quite a feature in the spring.

resemble in growth; chestnuts, large and noble trees for cool mountain climates; walnuts (ditto: seedling trees bear the best nuts, but take many years to bear; 'Wilson's Wonder' will fruit in about five years); hazelnuts; the majestic stone pine, *Pinus pinea*, source of the *pignolas* used in Italian cooking; and, for mild coastal places, the king of them all — the Queensland or macadamia nut. This is a stately evergreen tree, handsome in growth, foliage and flower, and the only native plant that white Australians eat. It is much grown in America, where it is called the California nut. Buy a named variety, selected to bear nuts that are less than impossible to crack, and give it the best soil you can.

ORGANIC

A chemist calls 'organic' any substance that, whether derived from the processes of life or not, contains carbon atoms arranged in a certain way — and that includes plastic! But for most of us the term denotes something that is indeed derived from once-living matter, and which is in its turn biodegradable. Thus grass clippings are an organic mulch, gravel is not; blood and bone is an organic fertiliser, but not super-phosphate.

An 'organic gardener' shuns all products of chemical factories, fertilising the ground with compost,

manure and the like, and controlling bugs and diseases (not always very effectively) with plant-derived sprays like TOBACCO or GARLIC WATER. Some enthusiasts can't resist nostalgia for what they call 'the good old days' and will insist on dragging in any sort of notion that they find in ancient and dusty books, so that ideas like gardening by the stars get mixed up in it. But the philosophy isn't as cranky as it sometimes sounds: fertilisers and pesticides *are* major polluters of the environment, and they don't do anything for the microscopic creatures on which the health and continued fertility of the soil depends. And we are a shockingly wasteful society, throwing out as garbage all sorts of things that should be recycled to the benefit of the soil.

Most of us aren't purist in our approach: we make compost and prefer manure to chemical fertilisers, but also use pesticides and fungicides, but as a last resort and with great circumspection.

It is a matter of temperament. If you are one of those people who can't abide the sight of a bug and demand that every flower in the garden and every vegetable that you bring to table be quite unblemished, then you will be reluctant to give up the use of chemicals to that end.

It isn't true that organically grown fruit and vegetables are more nutritious. They aren't. And whether they are worth the extra cost to buy at the markets is debatable. But if you grow your own, you have the comfort of knowing that they are as free from additives as may be.

ONIONS

I love onions, but have never found it worthwhile to grow my own: they take a long time (nearly a year) to produce, and I'd rather give the space to expensive luxuries like strawberries or mignonette lettuce. But spring onions, sometimes called (incorrectly) shallots, are a different matter. They are just onion seedlings, from seed sown much more thickly than the packet suggests, and pulled up when they are big enough to eat.

If you buy a bunch of spring onions and require only half for that meal, plant the rest in the garden, where they will thrive until required.

The onion's relative, GARLIC, is good value too.

ONION WEED

Lowly cousin of the onion, which it vaguely resembles on a small scale, *Nothoscordum inodorum* is not only totally devoid of charm — few weeds can make a garden look so unloved —

The onions are perhaps the royal family of vegetables. Here are leeks, shallots, spring onions, chives, garlic, and onions themselves, all members of the genus Allium.

This is what makes onion weed so pernicious — pull out the main plant, and all those babies detach themselves and get left behind to grow again.

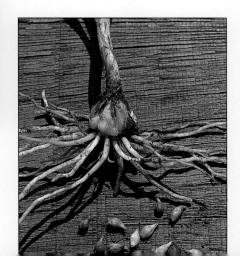

the dainty Chinese ground orchid (*Bletilla striata*) flowering every spring in a shaded, well-composted border. In my present garden in Sydney I can grow cymbidiums, zygopetalums, the lovely *Coelogyne cristata*, stanhopeas, a whole range of native orchids, and at least some slipper orchids, cattleyas and dendrobiums, their pots standing outside on a lightly shaded terrace, and the plants being brought indoors when they bloom to protect the delicate blossoms from the weather. Many of these will grow similarly in Melbourne, and Brisbane gardeners can add vandas and oncidiums to the list. Here, if

Orchid plants can be expensive, but don't let that put you off. None of the flowers in this mouth-watering display is beyond the owner of even a modest bush house. From front to back, they are miltonias, odontoglossums, and cymbidiums, the easiest of all.

The frilly hybrid cattleyas are the most glamorous of all orchids, but they are not difficult to grow. A greenhouse suits them best, but many will grow quite happily outdoors in southern Australia. Keep them on the dry side in winter or their roots will rot.

it is a perfect devil to get rid of. Not only will it shed seeds everywhere, it grows from clumps of bulbs, which invariably break up when you dig it up, leaving behind innumerable babies the size of grains of rice. And by the time you notice they are growing again, they have made a new generation of offsets. GLYPHOSATE will kill it, but remove any flower or seed heads and burn them, just in case.

ORCHIDS

The glamour (and costliness) of orchids seduces many people into thinking of them as needing to be pampered in heated greenhouses, where they will die the instant the gardener neglects some tiny detail of their fiendishly complex cultivation. But this is not so. True, having a greenhouse does extend your scope, but there is hardly a garden in this country where some pretty orchids couldn't grow quite happily out of doors. Even in Canberra I used to have

anywhere in gardening, local knowledge of what does best is indispensable. If you can't find your local orchid society in the phone book, ask at your local nursery.

It is difficult to generalise about so vast and diverse a group (the orchids are the largest family in the plant kingdom), but let us try.

Almost all the flower-shop orchids are EPIPHYTES, which means that in the wild they grow cradled in trees (and can be treated similarly in the garden, if your climate suits the ones you choose). It is for convenience that they are grown in pots, in specially prepared potting mixes based on such things as chopped up bark and sphagnum moss instead of soil. The various types prefer slightly different mixes, but all will insist on absolutely perfect drainage — whoever saw a bog halfway up a tree?

Most orchids have a distinct rest period each year, when they like to be kept on the dry side; it is ignoring this and drowning the poor plants that causes most trouble, but they like to be well watered and given some fertiliser (diluted MANURE WATER being ideal) while they are growing. Just what time of the year all this happens varies with the species, and the plants in a mixed collection will need individual treatment, which is one of the things that makes orchid growing look complicated.

Almost all like a little shade, but few need it really heavy. An orchid that doesn't get enough light may grow luxuriantly with rich green leaves, but it will flower only sparsely. Better to err on the side of too much light, even if the foliage ends up looking a bit pallid — orchid leaves are rarely all that exciting anyway.

If you do have a greenhouse, keep it well ventilated in summer (orchids hate stagnant air), and keep the temperatures from rocketing up with ventilation, syringing the plants with water, and shading the house. Even the true tropical orchids, like vandas and phalanopsis, suffer in temperatures over about 30°C.

Repotting and division is called for every so often, keeping the younger growths and giving away the older,

leafless 'back bulbs' (most orchids make fleshy, vaguely bulb-like stems called 'pseudo-bulbs'), which will come to life if they are repotted and will flower in a few years. Precisely when, and how often, to do this varies with the species; if you are faced with an orchid that is obviously outgrowing its pot and aren't sure what to do with it, you can simply transfer it to a bigger pot. Sometimes, as with some cattleyas, you will find the roots clinging to the pot, and it will be less distressing to the plant to simply replant it pot and all in the bigger pot. It may not be orthodox, but it has worked for me.

The main pests of orchids are SNAILS and CATERPILLARS, which love young orchid flower buds, and slaters, which nibble the tips of the roots. Snail bait will kill off the last as well as snails; for caterpillars, see the entry on them.

OXALIS

The Andean Indians eat the hazelnut-sized, sharply flavoured bulbs of oxalis, which they call *Oca*. They have a saying that 'a stew without oca is like a night without love', and with their silky pink or yellow flowers (the tall yellow one,

Oxalis pes-caprae, *the soursob, is a very pretty flower indeed, but it is a most pernicious weed, only too happy to take over the garden and choke everything else out.*

Oxalis pes-caprae, is sometimes called soursob, not to be confused with soursop, a kind of custard apple) and their clover-like leaves that close up at night, oxalis are rather charming.

But allow yourself to be beguiled, and you'll regret it, for oxalis shares onion weed's ability to proliferate alarmingly by seeds and clumps of bulbs that break up if you try to dig it out. Treat it the same way. There are a few creeping species that don't make bulbs, but in pulling them out you have to get out every bit, or there will be regrowth: not a heavy job, but one productive of bad language if the oxalis is entwined through the shoots of some desirable plant.

Some species, such as *O. enneaphylla* and *O. hirta*, are both very pretty and (relatively) non-invasive; they are great talking points in the garden. (Poor Mildred, she must have taken leave of her senses; fancy planting oxalis!) The nervous can try them as pot plants.

Propagation

If you've never looked in delighted anticipation at a tray of germinating seedlings, rich with promise of flowers or eatables to come, or stood in front of a shrub and thought of the friend who gave you the cutting years ago, or lifted a clump of some favourite perennial, knowing that soon you would have three or four where before you had only one, you've been missing out on a lot of the fun of gardening. And you've been spending more than you need: it takes a lot of money to buy enough plants to fill a garden.

The simplest plants to propagate are those like violets, strawberries and mint that enthusiastically make **runners:** you just have to wait for the runners to take root, detach the new plants and transfer them to their new homes. Indeed with these you may have to curtail their enthusiastic increase lest they prove INVASIVE. Many GROUNDCOVER plants fall into this category.

Next easiest are the herbaceous PERENNIALS and BULBS that multiply into clumps. At the usual planting time, you just dig up the whole lot, shake the soil off the roots, and **divide** the clump, assisting it, if need be, by cutting the rootstock with a sharp knife. (You can use secateurs if you promise to clean the dirt off immediately.) Unless you really need a large number of new plants, don't try to break the clump into little bits — often it will simply fall apart into conveniently sized new plants.

Rhododendrons are cheaper than they used to be, thanks to the technique of rooting cuttings under spray of artificial fog. In the old days, they had to be layered or grafted, both slow and expensive exercises.

So far, it has proved very difficult to propagate eucalypts in any other way than from seed, and seedlings tend to vary. Which can be maddening when your eagerly awaited scarlet flowering gum turns out to be pale pink. Recent research offers hope and it won't be too long before eucalypts can be cloned and you'll have a guaranteed red one.

LAYERING is easy too, but takes a little time, and you have to find a shoot that is low enough to bend down to the ground. It is a useful method of increasing climbing plants and shrubs like rhododendrons, azaleas and the laxer shrub roses, as well as soft fruit like raspberries — which will often layer themselves if they touch soft ground.

Also as easy as can be are the little bulbs (bulbils) that grow on the stems of the tiger lily and some of its relatives. Just remove them at flowering time and plant them; they take a couple of years to grow to flowering size. This must be the rarest of all ways of increasing a plant.

CUTTINGS can be either easy or difficult; it depends more on the individual plant's willingness to root than on the

TAKING CUTTINGS

1 To take a cutting, cut cleanly (a razor blade is useful) just below a leaf where the growth auxins and hormones are most active.

2 Take more cuttings than you need, and place in potting mix.

when the flower has fallen and the thorns break off cleanly), camellias, escallonias, grevilleas and their relatives, or daphne. Both types are best put in pots and given the warmth and humidity of the greenhouse or cold frame; if you don't have either, try enclosing the pot of cuttings entirely in a plastic bag and set it in a shady spot.

Deciduous shrubs and trees can be rooted from cuttings of the **mature** wood in late autumn or winter, which shouldn't need protection but will root fairly slowly. Often, they will grow from midsummer cuttings also, so you have a long season for experimenting. With all types, dipping the end of each cutting in rooting HORMONE can greatly increase your proportion of 'strikes', but it's always wise to take more cuttings than you need. Not all will strike, and only some of these will grow into sturdy plants.

Not all woody plants will grow readily from cuttings; eucalypts are impossible, rhododendrons notoriously difficult — but try anyway, you might just get a pleasant surprise! Try to take your cuttings only from young, flourishing plants; they seem to grow more readily than those from old and struggling ones. But never reject the offer of a cutting of a plant you want — it just might grow, even if it is officially the wrong type or the wrong time.

African violets and begonias can be grown from **leaf cuttings,** which are just leaves set in pots like any other cutting, and many plants will grow from **root cuttings.** These are simply pieces of root, buried in a sandy potting mix; top end up allows you more in the pot, but you can set them horizontally if you can't remember which end was which. Try them with acanthus, peonies (rather slow) and *Paulownia tomentosa*, the princess tree.

GRAFTING is really only for the dedicated gardener; it's a delicate operation, taking practice. If you fancy trying your

process itself, which is simple enough. You just take a piece of shoot, trim its base, remove any excess leaves, and set the bottom end in a coarsely sandy soil to make roots. There's less chance of bruising it if you make a hole with a chopstick first, and gently firm in the cutting. It's usually easiest to put your cuttings in a pot, which you can either enclose in a plastic bag to keep everything moist and humid, or place in the greenhouse if you have one.

The trick is knowing what sort of shoot to take.

Herbaceous plants, like dahlias, carnations and, should you want to increase a particular favourite, petunias and pansies, are grown from **slips** taken from the flowerless shoots that arise from the base of the plant, and root best in spring and early summer.

Soft-wooded and fast-growing shrubs, like fuchsias, lavender, rosemary or cistus, will root fastest from **softwood** cuttings taken from the ends of the shoots while they are still growing fairly actively, usually in late spring; but they will also grow from the **semi-mature** growths that are best for most evergreen shrubs. Take these about midsummer: the wood is ready when it is no longer soft, but firm enough to snap if you bend it sharply. (If it just bends, chances are it's too mature.) Try this type with roses (the wood is ready

Lemons are often grafted onto Poncirus trifoliata, *which helps them to endure the cold, but don't buy 'Meyer' this way — it isn't compatible and sooner or later will begin to die off. Choose seedling lemon roots if you have a choice.*

hand, start with easy things like cacti, where all you have to do is tie the scion (the top part of the finished plant) on to the understock (the plant that will provide the roots), and then graduate to budding roses — budding is the easiest type of grafting. Then you can investigate the pleasures of cleft grafting, veneer grafting and inarching. Camellia enthusiasts often become adept, as they can beg tiny scions from fellow camellians and see their new flowers sooner than from cuttings.

All of these fall into the category of what is called **asexual** or **vegetative** propagation, and they reproduce the character of the parent plant exactly. They are creating, or perpetuating a CLONE, and you should select your propagating material from a parent that you find desirable enough to perpetuate. Of course, you won't want to perpetuate a plant that is diseased, particularly one with virus disease.

GROWING PLANTS FROM SEED

Nature does most of its propagation from seed, and there are few plants that you can't grow from seed, if you are patient — many trees and perennials take several years to grow to flowering size. Vegetative propagation from mature plants is usually quicker, but seed does have the great advantage that VIRUS diseases rarely affect it, and so clean stocks can be created and maintained. And it is often easier to find seeds of rare species than developed plants.

Seed has the disadvantage that the seedlings won't be quite identical to their parents, but nurserymen select their strains carefully and the results from a packet of zinnias or cauliflowers should be what you were expecting. If you save your own seed — and apart from the F1 hybrids it's worth

Dahlia tubers can be divided, but you must cut the clump apart with great care, because the 'eyes' are on the crown, the stubs of last year's shoots, and unless each tuber has a piece of this attached, it won't grow. This is the tree dahlia, D. imperialis.

Impatiens must be the easiest of all plants to propagate from cuttings — just pick a bunch, stand them in a cup of warmish water and they will make roots in a fortnight.

It may be faster to grow lilies from division than from seed, but seed is safer — lilies are subject to fatal virus diseases and seedlings start with a clean bill of health. Oriental hybrids (this is 'Stargazer') are inclined to take eighteen months to germinate. Just keep the pot moist and be patient.

Bearded iris rhizomes can be trimmed into quite small pieces, each with a fan of leaves (trim these back), but bigger sections settle down again faster. Divide immediately after flowering.

doing — then you need to be selective and save only from your best plants.

Large seeds, like nasturtiums, peas or sweet corn, are the easiest to grow. Simply put them where you want your plants and cover them with their own thickness of fine soil, watering until they come up. If you like, you can lay a piece of old hessian over your seed bed as a mulch and to break the force of the hose, but remove it the instant you see signs of germination. Put two or three seeds at each station, and remove the weaker seedlings.

Smaller seeds are best sown in containers; you can use flower pots, the punnets seedlings are sold in, or even egg cartons. The potting mix needs to be free from lumps and free-draining; you don't want your seeds or tiny seedlings rotting. A half-and-half mix of sand and ordinary potting mix should do. Sow your seeds thinly, cover them to their own depth — with very small seeds this means only the

finest dusting of dry soil — and water gently until they come up. Tiny seedlings are prone to 'damping off', a form of mildew, and it's worth watering them with a dilute fungicide when they first appear. Making sure they have fresh air and don't get waterlogged are the best preventatives. As soon as the baby plants are large enough to handle, 'prick them out' into other containers or a nursery bed, setting them about 5 centimetres apart, to grow on until they are big enough to take the rough and tumble of the open garden. They will need regular watering, and meticulous protection from snails.

All seeds call for gentle handling, but the very finest, like those of begonias and petunias, are fiddly to handle, and the seed merchants often pellet them to give you something big enough to play with. If there are any special things you have to do with the particular seeds, like soaking them in water first, you can expect the packet to tell you — follow its directions carefully! The best place to keep seeds that are not going to be used immediately is the refrigerator. And be patient; while some seeds come up in a matter of days, some take quite a long time.

PARTERRE

The French word, literally 'on the ground', denotes the elaborately patterned beds edged with clipped box found in grand French and Italian formal gardens. They were not always filled with flowers — sometimes colour was provided with different colours of gravel. (In France, at least, this can look better than it sounds.) It is the height of pretentiousness to give the title to an ordinary flower bed.

Paths need not be made of hard paving; this one is of tanbark. Its faintly rustic air suits the informal style of this garden (the flowers are daylilies).

PATHS

A path between two blocks of vegetable in the kitchen garden can be as narrow as you can squeeze down, as it serves only for access to the plants, but one linking parts of the garden needs to be generous and comfortable — two people can't stroll and talk in a space less than about a metre and a half wide. Of course, this should allow for the growth of nearby plants — you don't want your hat knocked off as you go past.

Whatever the surface — bricks, stone, gravel, grass, concrete — it needs to be even so that you don't trip, and non-slippery in any weather.

Wood, bricks and stone, particularly in shady spots and in prolonged rain, are prone to get covered in black slimy algae which is not only unsightly but also as slippery as glass. It can be got rid of, at least temporarily, by scrubbing gently with an old, stiff brush and household bleach or a pale blue solution of copper sulphate. The copper sulphate (buy it at the chemist) is less likely to upset any plants it gets splashed on, and its effect lasts longer, but it isn't as cheap as bleach and it is apt to leave the bricks a strange colour.

PEONIES

These splendid late spring flowers come in two versions: the ordinary peonies or peony roses, which are long-lived herbaceous perennials for cold climates, and the even more sumptuous tree peonies, which in their native China are called the King of Flowers. These aren't trees at all, but rosebush-sized, deciduous shrubs with wood nearly as soft as a geranium's. They are more often dreamt about than seen, for they are fabulously expensive. This isn't because they are difficult to grow — they will flourish, in rich soil and light shade, wherever the winter is cool enough for daffodils — but because they are extremely tricky and slow to propagate. This is done by grafting a scion of the tree peony onto a piece of herbaceous peony root, in the hope that it will keep the tree peony alive until it eventually makes roots of its own. Failure is common and success takes time; even the wispy plant you take out a second mortgage to buy will be three or four years old.

It isn't often that you find tree peonies as named varieties in Australia, but one to look out for is the lemon-yellow 'Alice Harding', said to be the best for mild-winter climates. There are many plants like this, whose price tag represents difficulty in the nursery rather than in the garden; before you invest the money, find out if the plant you fancy is one of them. (The black kangaroo paw is one, some rhododendrons and small conifers are others.)

Tree peonies are often sold simply by colour, but are no less beautiful for lacking a pedigree; these two beauties were nameless.

PERENNIALS

In strict scientific usage, a perennial is any plant that lives for three years or more — sometimes very many more. The term thus embraces trees and shrubs, but when gardeners speak of perennials, we almost always mean those clumpy plants that don't have permanent woody stems as trees and shrubs do.

Some, the **herbaceous perennials**, die down to a resting crown or clump of tubers each year: dahlias, delphiniums, cannas, rhubarb and chrysanthemums are a few familiar ones from an almost endless list. Others are **evergreen**, like some irises and daylilies, carnations, Japanese anemones, and many indoor plants, like the spathyphyllums, also known as peace lilies. Geraniums, marguerites, sage and the gorgeous pride of Madeira (*Echium fastuosum*) are actually soft-wooded shrubs (the botanical term is sub-shrubs), but we think of them as evergreen perennials too, and usually plant them with the others.

With so large and diverse a tribe, it is impossible to generalise about how they are grown — some like sun, others shade, some plenty of water, others less — but all appreciate generous preparation of their sites with cultivation and compost: they will have to live there for some years. Most are propagated by DIVISION of their crowns (or tubers) while they are resting, but unless you want to increase your stock in a hurry, this is only necessary if they get so crowded that their flowering suffers.

Just because botanists (and gardening writers) like to keep their

The high season for perennial flowers is late spring, when it is easy to achieve displays like this (the flowers are mostly bearded irises and oriental poppies) — keeping the show going for the rest of the summer and autumn calls for planning beforehand, to include later-blooming perennials and annuals.

classes of plants separated, there's no reason to do that in the garden; perennials can consort quite happily with annuals, shrubs, or bulbs in a flower bed, as well as looking splendid in plantings on their own.

PERGOLAS

The actual structure of a pergola is a question of architecture rather of gardening proper, and while we usually attach it to the house as a sort of vine-roofed verandah — and useful it can be too for controlling the sun — there's no reason why it can't be a free-standing structure (what the Americans call an arbour or a lanai), or cover a path to make a shady tunnel. Whatever it be built of, let its structure be strong, for a vine in full growth and wet with rain is heavy.

Detached from the house, a pergola clad with vines can bring shade to the garden faster than trees can. The wisteria here was planted only three years ago.

The Romans grew grapes on theirs, for both the fruit and the pleasure of sitting in their shade, and we can follow their example. But wisteria is a classic choice too, considerately hanging its flowers below the structure where they can be admired. (Keep it in bounds by summer pruning, cutting the whippy growths back to three or four leaves.) Both grape vine and wisteria drop their leaves to let in the winter sun, but in the subtropics you may prefer an evergreen like an allamanda, the purple wreath (*Petraea volubilis*), or one of the bignonia tribe,

for year-round shade. They will probably need regular thinning, or there will be a mound of branches with all the flowers on top, and nothing to look at from beneath. The daintier growers, like the wonga-wonga vine (*Pandorea*) and the Carolina jessamine don't have this bad habit, but they don't cast much shade; they would be a good choice if the structure itself were so handsome that you didn't want to conceal it too much. But do avoid bougainvillea and roses (except trained to the pillars); getting up among their thorny branches to tend

them or to paint the pergola is no fun. For instant shade while the permanent vines are coming on, you could grow moonflowers or the cup and saucer vine (*Cobaea scandens*), both very rapid growers from seed sown in spring; or shadecloth could do temporary duty. Fix it to the underside of the beams (drawing pins will do) or you'll have trouble removing it from under the vines later.

You're not restricted to climbers; fruit trees (apples or pears) can be trained to conform to the structure, and the English make tunnels of laburnum. But this is a much slower business, and pruning is a constant job.

pH

The pH scale of 1 to 14, defined (with scientific precision if not clarity) as *the negative logarithm of the concentration of hydrogen ions in a solution* is the measure of ACIDITY or ALKALINITY. A measure of 1 indicates an acid strong enough to dissolve anything it touches, one of 14 an alkali of similar ferocity; 7 is perfectly neutral, like pure water. The scale applies not only to soil (or more precisely to the soil moisture) but to any solution — cosmetics manufacturers are keen to ensure that their creams and ointments match the pH of the skin. Each step is ten times as large as the next, so that a soil of pH 5 is ten times as acid as one of pH 6. Most soils fall somewhere between 5.5 and 8.6 or so, with a neutral or slightly acid reaction (say 7.5 to 6) being ideal for most plants. It is rather impressive to know the pH of one's soil, and you can buy kits to test it or have the Department of Agriculture do it for you for a small fee, but most of us don't bother, learning from experience (our own or the neighbours') what sort of plants do well.

PHOSPHORUS

The second of the big three elements that the soil has to supply to plants, and which the gardener needs to replenish regularly, phosphorus is essential for strong stems, continuing growth, and proper development of flowers and fruit. It never occurs except as various compounds, and as most of these are insoluble, it is still something of a mystery how plants get their phosphorus out of the soil. SUPERPHOSPHATE is the standard phosphorus fertiliser, but BLOOD AND BONE and bone meal (or bone flour) will supply it too. Australian soils tend to be deficient in the element, and many native plants (especially the protea family, the grevilleas, hakeas and their relatives) are very sensitive to overdoses of it. Don't use super-phosphate on them; content yourself with compost or manure. See also NITROGEN, NPK, POTASSIUM.

PHYTOPHTHORA

A relative of the potato blight (*Phytophthora infestans*) that led to the great famines in Ireland in the 1840s, *P. cinnamomi*, the cinnamon root rot or die-back fungus that is wreaking such havoc in the jarrah forests of Western Australia, can be a real nuisance in gardens too. It lives in wet soil, and can infest the roots of many plants — most natives are susceptible, camellias also — killing off the root tips so that the plant dies of thirst, often in a matter of days. Once it starts to die there is little that can be done; improving the drainage, adding some ground limestone and following up with a drench of Dexon (a potent and poisonous fungicide) will help discourage the fungus. It would be wise to replant with a resistant species (most plants that naturally grow in damp ground are candidates), and to scrupulously avoid transferring infected soil to other parts of the garden. Cinnamon fungus is one of those things that one wouldn't wish on one's worst enemy.

PHYTOTOXIC

A word you sometimes come across in the more erudite gardening books; it simply means 'poisonous to plants'. Weedkillers are, by definition, but other chemicals can be too if they are used carelessly, by being sprayed on too strongly, for instance. If you are mixing

The famous double avenue of pleached limes at Sissinghurst Castle in England. The lime or linden (Tilia europaea) finds most parts of Australia a bit hot for its liking, but if you fancy re-creating the picture there is still a fair choice — any tree that will stand the regular and firm pruning needed could be tried.

sprays (insecticide with fungicide for instance), be sure they are compatible. Phone the manufacturer to check if need be.

PINCHING

Sometimes called **tip pruning,** this is done to plants like lavender, small-flowered chrysanthemums and many native shrubs to make them bushy. All you do is pinch out the tips of the young growth, stopping of course when the plant shows signs of wanting to flower.

Pinching back the tip of a growing shoot to encourage bushiness. You can use scissors if you prefer.

PLEACHING

Pleaching is a bit like ESPALIERING: the branches of a tree (or more usually a row of them) are trained while they are still young and flexible to a flat plane, to create a narrow wall of foliage, standing on the clean trunks as though on a row of stilts. This is easiest if you put up temporary wires to train branches to; after a year or so they will be firm enough to be self-supporting. Pruning thereafter simply consists of removing any branches that try to grow away from the 'wall'.

PLEACHING

1 *The young trees are planted at the foot of the wires.*

2 *As the trees grow, the branches are tied in to the wires, and any that are trying to grow forward are removed.*

POISONOUS PLANTS

The list of poisonous garden plants is a long one: delphiniums, daffodils, poinsettias, frangipani, lily of the valley, philodendrons, rhododendrons, to name just a few. But it shouldn't be cause for alarm; poisoning by garden plants is actually very rare. Which, on reflection, isn't so surprising — most of us don't go around the garden snacking on the flowers.

Toddlers do, though, and while it's easy to say they shouldn't be let out in the garden unsupervised until they are past the stage of tasting anything unfamiliar, it's only prudent to keep notoriously poisonous plants like oleanders (both the common one and its relative, the even more toxic yellow oleander or *Thevetia*) out of parts of the garden to which they are allowed access, and to keep all indoor plants well out of reach. Fortunately most poisonous plants announce the fact by being very bitter; the ones to watch particularly are those that have attractive berries like lily of the valley, arums, and the ornamental capsicums

Lily of the valley has been used in traditional medicine but it is dangerously poisonous to the nibbler.

It is a technique best suited to a very formal, architectural sort of garden. You often see screens of pleached lindens in small gardens in London, and the idea could be copied here, where a tall screen is needed without either giving the yard over entirely to trees or erecting a forbiddingly tall trellis to clad with vines.

Almost any tree that will take pruning would be suitable for pleaching. European limes and hornbeams are traditional, but you could also use flowering pears, fruit trees, one of the very big hibiscus, like 'Agnes Galt', or even bougainvillea.

Oleanders are poisonous, but so bitter that even goats won't try to eat them. Don't, however, put oleander twigs on your barbeque fire, let alone use them as skewers. It has happened!

(not actually poisonous, but *very* chili-pepper-hot); those that have sticky sap that might get rubbed into eyes (poinsettias, euphorbias and oleanders); or which have seeds that a child might swallow (the yellow oleander, wisteria, *Melia azederach*, the

white cedar). If you have the slightest suspicion that a child might have eaten something nasty, don't delay: take them to the hospital at the first sign of unease.

It's a good precaution to wash your hands after handling any plant you are not certain of to avoid any possibility of poisoning.

The flip side of all this is that a surprising number of plants we wouldn't think of eating are in fact edible: dahlias, tulips, daylilies, roses, cotoneasters, among others.

POISONS

Prudence dictates that *any* chemical you buy for the garden, no matter what reassurances may be printed on the package, be treated as a dangerous poison, and kept safely away from children and pets, on a high shelf in a locked shed if need be, and that you wash your hands after using them. And what about all the household things like bleach and detergent? They need careful storage too. See the feature on SAFETY IN THE GARDEN.

Pruning

WHY PRUNE?

Pruning is a kind of surgery that we perform on plants, with the aim of encouraging them to grow in the way we want. It isn't usually an essential job and the notes you see in garden books advising you to 'prune after flowering' or 'prune in winter' should be read as meaning 'that's when you prune if you want to'. Nature manages to get by quite well without pruning, and often all we need to do to assist her is to remove dead and sickly wood, dead flowers and so on, more for the sake of neatness than anything else. But in addition, we might prune for several reasons:

◆ To **allow light and air** into a plant that has grown so bushy that the inside branches and leaves are being shaded out. This might involve THINNING the plant's structure overall, or (more usually) simply removing the weak and possibly sickly shoots from the inside. This is the only sort of pruning that naturally shapely plants like camellias need. It is also the main reason for pruning fruit trees: we want the fruit to develop on the lower, easy-to-reach branches as well as just the top ones that hog the sunlight. Thinning the branches also allows wind to flow through the plant, and reduces the possibility of damage (or the whole thing blowing over) in storms.

◆To **direct and control growth**, encouraging strong branches to grow in a well-spaced arrangement, or to make the plant more bushy and shapely. Often, we want to remove shoots and branches that won't bear much in the way of flowers or fruit in order to make the plant concentrate its energy on those that will, as when we shorten the whippy growths of WISTERIA or grape vines, or remove worn-out branches on ROSES, weigelas, or philadelphus (mock oranges). Hibiscus too often make long, whippy branches that carry few blooms, and by shortening these we encourage new shoots from low down on the bush, making it more compact and flowery. Most of your pruning will be directed to these ends, but it's easy to get obsessive about it: the plant is just as anxious to flower and fruit as you are to have it do so, and left to its own devices will do quite a good job. Just look at an ancient unpruned rosebush covered in bloom, or a neglected apple tree laden with fruit! Start this or any kind of pruning by removing any dead and obviously weak or sickly branches, and then stand back to see if more is really necessary.

◆ To **repair damage**, by removing branches that have broken off (in storms maybe), or those that have died from other causes, such as borers or other insects, or from disease. Here you simply cut back to sound wood, either back to the plant's main framework or to a point where a sound branch is growing. Often, two branches will be rubbing against one another, chafing their bark. The weaker is best removed. Sometimes the damage has been caused by other people's

---

PRUNING TO REMOVE OLD WOOD

1 *Hydrangeas can be much improved if you cut some of the oldest growth out each year. Prune in late winter to early spring.*

2 *Cut away the old stems — rough looking branches with side shoots. Cut to just above a bud.*

3 *The finished result. The plant may look like a plucked chicken but it will soon fill out. Spring flowering shrubs like mock oranges or weigela are treated the same way.*

Pruning a hydrangea, leaving the shoots that haven't yet flowered and removing those that have. This can be done either immediately the flowers fade, or in winter, allowing you to enjoy the pleasing colours that the old flowers assume in the autumn.

1 Use a pruning saw to remove a branch that has been broken or become weak or overcrowded. Make the first cut upwards, a little way from the trunk, to remove most of the branch.

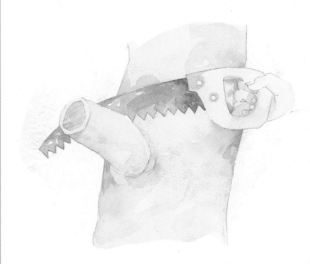

2. Cut the remaining part of the branch away using a downward cut, flush with the trunk.

careless pruning, usually in the form of indiscriminate 'cutting back' so that there are too many crowded new shoots and branches. Here the task is to select the best of these, placed so that when they grow, the plant's proper form will be restored. This is largely a matter of artistic judgment. Often the need for cutting back has resulted from poor judgment in selecting a plant that is simply too big for its position, and it may be worth considering whether to remove it altogether, or to adjust its surroundings to allow room for it. (You might, for instance, consider changing the line of a path which is being crowded by a too-big but otherwise desirable shrub.)

◆ To **renew a plant entirely**. Sometimes the only way to deal with a vastly overgrown shrub — say, a rosebush, or a lilac, even an azalea — that is dissipating its energies in a mass of twigs is simply to cut it almost to the ground in winter, forcing it to make strong young branches from the base. But this is drastic surgery indeed, and you must

compensate the plant for the loss of its branches by fertilising it heavily in the spring. Some thinning of the new shoots may be called for, but this can wait until the following winter when you see what the plant is going to do. Don't be surprised if it takes a couple of years to come back into full bearing again. You can do the same annually to shrubs that tend to die back a bit and look scruffy after flowering, like poinsettias and the chinese plumbago (*Ceratostigma*), but there is no need to do it to crepe myrtles; to my eye at least, the resulting long rods of growth crowned with huge blobs of flowers are no compensation for the loss of the graceful natural shape of the tree adorned with smaller clusters.

Beware of cutting too much foliage out of the crown of an evergreen tree when you prune it, as the bark on the trunk and branches might get sunburned. Avocados are especially prone to sunburn, and so are citrus — hence the Mediterranean tradition of whitewashing the trunks of lemon trees.

◆ To **create a pleasing artificial form**, as when you shear a HEDGE, shape a piece of TOPIARY, or train a plant as an ESPALIER or STANDARD. The rather rarer PLEACHING and POLLARDING come under this heading too. And so, when you think of it, does mowing the lawn. You might also thin a tree or shrub for purely aesthetic reasons, removing sufficient twigs and foliage to show the lines of the branches, something at which the Japanese are the masters.

◆ To **establish a sound framework** in the first couple of years of the life of a tree. This is especially important with fruit trees, where you want to end up with a pyramidal form so that sun gets to all the branches, but most deciduous trees benefit from similar training too.

THE SURGEON'S SKILLS

Having decided you want to prune a branch, the rules are few. Gather together your tools. I find all I ever need are secateurs, long-handled loppers for wood too big for secateurs, and a coarse-toothed pruning saw for anything that's too big for the loppers. (A hand saw is slower, and harder work, than a chain saw, but chainsaws are heavy,

WHEN TO PRUNE?

The rule of thumb is immediately after flowering, unless you are expecting fruit to follow, when winter is the time. This does mean winter for most things, when the plant is dormant (or at least not very active), but watch for spring-flowering shrubs like philadelphus, the various spring blossoms, old-fashioned roses, forsythia and such, which form their flower buds on shoots they made in the previous summer. Here the temptation to tidy up the winter twigginess can be great, but you should resist it, or you'll be cutting away your flowers. With these, you might like to combine pruning with cutting generous branches of flowers for the house, choosing the oldest and twiggiest, then finishing off the job (by removing the just-bloomed branches back to a strong new shoot) as the bloom fades, but before the new growth begins in earnest. This needn't be an annual job, as it usually takes a couple of years before the flowering wood gets so twiggy that blooming falls off and the plant needs a tidy-up again. The same schedule applies to azaleas and deciduous magnolias, though they rarely need to be pruned, being naturally shapely. Summer-

'Cloud pruning' is a technique devised by the Japanese and used on small conifers, azaleas and such. The idea is that snow gathers on the almost horizontal 'clouds' of foliage to artistic effect. In mild climates, the technique, which is a kind of TOPIARY is useful in giving an authenticity to a Japanese-style garden.

Pruning a big tree is skilled and dangerous work . Notice how this fellow is attached to the tree by a safety rope, almost like a mountain climber. It is best to hire a professional for work on this scale, rather than take the risk of an accident yourself — a broken leg would cost more than the tree surgeon's fees.

noisy things, best left to professional tree-loppers and choppers of firewood.) Whatever tools you use, make sure they are *sharp*: a plant will suffer more from being torn about by dull blades than by wrongly placed cuts. That gives us the second rule: make your cuts cleanly, so as to give the plant the best chance of healing its wound. And third, cut back to where growth is going to come. Sometimes you can see the tiny growth bud on the stem, either in the axil (the 'armpit' of a leaf, or where a leaf once was) or if you can't cut there, it's best to cut back to just above a branch you want to save or to the main stem. Leaving stubs to die back not only looks unsightly, it invites rot and other problems.

Each species, and indeed each individual plant, is different; study your plants, learn to understand how they grow, and you won't have any trouble mastering the art of pruning — it is an art, as much as a science.

Bush roses (this is 'Apricot Nectar') need annual pruning to keep them youthful and full of flowers. Around the middle of July, cut dead and elderly branches right out, and shorten the remainder by about a third. No need to make the bush symmetrical, spring growth will fill it out.

1 *Many shrubs tend to fill up with old, worn out branches whose removal will let in light and air to the young ones. Removing old wood like this is the only pruning most old fashioned and shrub roses need.*

2 *To tidy up an evergreen shrub like an azalea or Abelia grandiflora, simply shorten any overgrown branches back to the main outline.*

3 *If you can't find growth buds to cut back to, cut the branch you want to remove right back to another one.*

4 *If a shrub is really getting overgrown, you can cut it back hard, preferably late in the winter. But be careful if you remove all the foliage like this: some shrubs like rosemary, most conifers, and many natives, won't grow back from old wood. With shrubs like lilac, camellias, or azaleas, the plant may skip a season's flowering while it rebuilds itself.*

Holding secateurs. The anvil of secateurs and loppers bruises as it cuts. Hold them the right way up, so that the bruise is on the bit you cut off!

flowering shrubs can be pruned in winter, as they mostly bloom on the shoots they make in spring, but it's wise to leave subtropical things like oleanders and hibiscus until the weather begins to warm up, so they don't have to cope with the shock of pruning in the cold.

You can do any needed THINNING or trimming of over-long shoots in late summer, when your tree or shrub is in full leaf, but don't cut as much as you might in winter, or you run the risk of newly un-shaded bark getting sunburned. But never, never, prune *anything* (except for the gentlest PINCHING) when it is in active growth and the sap is running, or you risk having the poor plant bleed to death. Dead branches can, of course, be removed at any time, as you notice them.

POLLARDING

More often seen in city streets than in gardens, pollarding is pruning the branches of a tree back to stumps each year, to control its size. It completely alters the character of the tree, turning it into a ball of leaves on a trunk. The places on the branches where each year's shoots are cut back eventually develop gnarled knobs of wood, which some people think look characterful and others hideous.

If you have ever cut back a crepe myrtle as the books usually suggest (you needn't; the hard cutting is only to force unnaturally large flower heads) you have been pollarding it.

POLLINATION

Even if your parents didn't tell you about the birds and the bees, you no doubt know about them by now, but it's surprising how easy it is to forget that if we want fruit the flowers have to be pollinated first. Usually the bees will handle the job for you, but if there aren't many about (citrus trees sometimes flower in cool weather when the bees stay inside), you can pollinate by hand, simply brushing over the flowers with a soft artist's paintbrush to transfer the pollen. Spraying tomato flowers with water will help the fruit to set.

Some fruit trees, notably apples, pears, cherries and almonds, have to receive pollen from a different tree. So you have to have two trees, of different varieties (all the trees of the same variety being a CLONE). Any good nursery list will tell you which varieties are compatible with each other. Sometimes you can buy the two budded onto the same tree, but you need to be careful in the early days with your pruning, lest you accidentally remove one altogether. Bees have no inhibitions about fences; if you and a neighbour both want to plant an apple tree, you might choose to plant compatible varieties and share the pollen. Or, as an alternative, you might swap a few sprays of blossoms with a friend, just putting them in a bucket of water under the tree.

POTASSIUM

The third of the big three elements in plant nutrition, potassium is important in plants' immune systems; a shortage shows up in stunted growth, browning of the leaf edges, and pallid flowers. It never occurs pure in nature, but is always combined with oxygen and other elements, such as sulphur; potassium compounds are usually called (rather loosely) potash. The element is important in giving resistance to cold. If you fertilise in autumn, cut back on nitrogen and give a little extra potash. Potassium sulphate or nitrate are the usual inorganic sources; ASH contains much potassium too. Potassium compounds are highly soluble in water, so keep any fertiliser containing them quite dry. Sometimes prolonged heavy rain will leach potassium from the soil and, as a result, you'll see mild deficiency symptoms. In such cases as these the application of a very light sprinkling of potassium sulphate (no more than about a third of the recommended dose) will help until the soil balances itself again. See also NPK.

PRUNING COMPOUND

Most books on gardening tell you that when you prune off a branch bigger than about 8 to 10 centimetres, you should paint the wound with pruning compound (also known as pruning paint) to seal it against possible rot. But recent research suggests that the practice may do more harm than good, by interfering with the plant's ability to heal itself. So as long as your cuts are cleanly and properly made (see the feature on PRUNING) you can regard brushing them with pruning compound as optional. Which is just as well, as the stuff is not easy to find.

On the other hand, a large cut on a branch can look unattractive: a great white scar against the trunk of your tree. It will weather to a grey colour soon enough, but you can quite safely touch it up with a little black ink in the meantime if you wish to make it less obtrusive.

QUANTITIES

Fertiliser packets have the irritating habit of telling you to spread so many grams per square metre, which is all very scientific and precise, but can you see yourself going around the garden with a bag of fertiliser in one hand and a tape measure and a pair of scales in the other? Normally, one sprinkles an artificial fertiliser on the ground to make a whitish look — like a cook *lightly* flouring a baking pan. But if you want to be more precise in applying chemicals to the soil (fertiliser isn't cheap, and a too-heavy application can be an overdose), try marking out a square metre on an old tarpaulin or such, measuring out the specified quantity on the kitchen scales and sprinkling it on that to see what it looks like. Once you have tested the quantities, you will soon be able to sprinkle your fertiliser by eye.

Soil conditioners and mulches can be treated in the same way: spread a sample to the suggested depth or quantity on your 'standard square metre'. It's alarming how the needed amounts of these build up, even to truckloads!

Sprays (insecticides and fungicides) only need to be applied sufficiently to wet the leaves; runoff is a waste and excess chemicals in the garden can be harmful.

If you have trouble sowing fine seeds evenly, one way of making the job easier is to bulk them up by mixing them with fine breadcrumbs or sand.

RAKING

Raking up leaves or grass clippings is a simple enough job, if tedious — and painful if you leave the rake tines up and step on them so that it flies up and hits you in the face. A bamboo or soft-tined rake will do the job here, but a steel-tined rake is useful to have for

Before you are tempted to copy one of the famous raked-sand gardens of Japan, remember that the raking has to be done daily; a spiritual exercise for a Zen monk, it is likely to prove a bore to the unenlightened.

preparing a bed to receive seeds or seedlings. Raking over the dug soil breaks the clods up finely enough to make everything ready. You can then rake stones out of your way.

Don't let leaves lie too thick on the lawn, or they will deprive the grass of light. Most mowers will cope with a light sprinkling: no need to rake before mowing unless the leaves really are thick.

Gravel looks neatest if you rake its surface over every so often, as foot traffic is apt to make it uneven. You can rake it into wavy patterns, Japanese style, if you wish; light bamboo rakes are used in Japan.

A stiff broom is best for sweeping up leaves from hard paving; rakes clatter.

ROOT PRUNING

If a shrub in a tub begins to outgrow its quarters and get pot-bound, one way of avoiding having to evict it to a larger container is to prune its roots. This is simple in theory: tip the plant out, shave 3 or 4 centimetres off the outside of the root ball with a very sharp knife, and replant. New roots will

grow where the old ones were cut and get the benefit of the fresh soil. A refinement is to prune only half the roots this year, the other half next year. In practice it is a cumbersome job if the plant is large, and a container like a VERSAILLES TUB with its false bottom (you could adapt a wine barrel on the same lines) makes life easier.

Pruning the roots to create a more compact root ball is a needed pre-liminary to TRANSPLANTING an established tree or shrub. Cut a narrow trench all around the plant, with a spade sharpened for the job, fill in with fine potting type soil, and when the new fine roots grow (allow a full year if you can) the plant is ready for lifting.

If you are faced with an apple or pear tree that puts all its energy into growth rather than flowering, you can try pruning its roots in the same way (but without transplanting it) with the aim of shocking it into flower and fruit. But don't try the trick on a citrus tree; it will simply resent it.

ROOT ROT
see PHYTOPHTHORA

sunshine for at least half the day, in the best soil you have. Prepare it a couple of months before planting time (the winter) by digging in as much compost as you can. They don't, despite folklore, really need clay: any sort of soil will suit, except for the sandiest, though even there the excellent hybrids of *Rosa rugosa* will flourish.

Half your success comes from choosing varieties that suit your area, and here a rose specialist can advise you, or you can seek the advice of your local rose society. Don't pine for varieties that mightn't like you; there are so many no one can grow them all anyway. The reds and pinks are usually easier to please than the yellows and oranges. In warm, humid-summer climates, consider the fragrant old tea roses, which the Victorians considered the most beautiful of all. Most bush roses can be planted about a metre apart; if you want to grow other flowers among the roses to hide their bad legs, do remember to allow space for them.

Pruning isn't as difficult as people make it sound, and isn't even all that necessary; a rosebush will cope quite

▲ Climbing or pillar roses can make a spectacular feature in the garden.

◀ Rosa rugosa *grows wild on the seashore in its native Japan, and even on sandy soils makes a lusty, handsome shrub. There are a number of varieties available, with single or double flowers over a long season. This one is the fragrant 'Roseraie de l'Hay'.*

ROSES

There is a great mystique about roses, perhaps starting from the fact that they are the only common plant that is always grafted and sold BARE-ROOT, and because they seem to need special treatment from the time you buy them. But they aren't at all difficult to grow. Give them a sunny spot, with full

▲ The Tea Roses feature exquisitely formed blooms and delicate colours. This one is 'Jean Ducher'; like most of its class, it does well in humid-summer climates.

▶ Standard roses are not a special class, but ordinary bush roses budded on long stems, which allow other flowers to grow beneath them. Here the scarlet 'Showbiz' is underplanted with snapdragons.

ROSES

well left to itself, at least for a couple of years. Just cut out any branches that are obviously dead or on the way out, and shorten the remainder by about a third, towards the end of winter. Follow with a thorough spraying with a complete rose spray to clean up any bugs and fungi lurking from last year. Then a mulch of compost or nicely rotted manure should set them up for the coming season. If you then give the bushes a light sprinkling of blood and bone as each lot of flowers fades, to encourage more, that is all the fertilising they will need.

Trim off the spent flowers as they fade, and keep the bushes well watered through the summer to keep them growing steadily. And watch out for APHIDS, MILDEW and BLACK SPOT. Other plagues are rare, and the only one to fear is wilt, a fatal and incurable virus which makes the stems go quite black and the shoots wilt. If you suspect it, take an affected branch to your nursery to confirm the diagnosis before destroying the infected plant.

Sometimes the understock will make unwanted suckers, which will look quite different from the cultivated rose. Rip (don't cut) them out at their source, but don't confuse them with the valuable watershoots that come from the base of the plant. If in doubt, watch for the flowers.

That's all there is to it!

SCALE

Garden designers have borrowed the architects' term 'in scale' or 'of human scale' to mean that everything is in proportion and comfortable for people, but whereas a giant building might seem oppressive, a giant tree in a forest might not. It might be out of scale and overwhelming in a small garden, but don't forget that the outdoors is a big place: the grand piano seems less imposing on the lawn than it does in the living-room.

SCALE INSECTS

These attack roses, citrus or young eucalypts, protecting themselves against enemies and insecticides beneath a shield of white wax. The scales are usually easy to see, sometimes covering the stems from end to end. The time-honoured remedy is to spray with white oil, which dissolves the wax and suffocates the insect. This is awkward stuff, liable to harm foliage in hot weather. A small infestation can be killed by brushing it lavishly with methylated spirit to the same effect. There are black scales, too. They are less common but may be dealt with in the same way.

White scale on a young eucalypt. An infestation as bad as this can cripple the tree and should be dealt with promptly. Fortunately, the insect is less of a bother once the tree is established and growing strongly.

It is hard to give rules for designing in scale, but here everything, the steps, the flowers on either side, and the tree that arches overhead, are just right. Try imagining any of them much larger or smaller — the harmony would be quite spoilt.

SCENT

The fragrance of flowers and leaves is impossible to photograph and difficult to convey in words, so it is easily overlooked when one is choosing plants from books and catalogues. People's perception of fragrance varies: what to one is rich and sweet may seem heavy and overpowering to another. And some people simply can't smell certain flowers. My mother couldn't smell violets, even the most richly fragrant (and I inherited her disability), and I know people who find brown boronia quite odourless.

Favourite plants with scented flowers
Roses
Lilies
Carnations
Heliotrope
Violets
Brown boronia (*B. megastigma*)
JASMINE, of all kinds
Jonquils
Osmanthus
GARDENIAS
Orange blossom
Lily of the valley

Favourite plants with scented leaves
Eau-de-cologne mint
Rosemary
Lavender
Cistus
Gum leaves of many kinds
Thyme
Lemon-scented verbena
Moschosma (*Iboza riparia*)
Catmint
Most pines (*Pinus*)

S C E N T

It's not entirely true that hybridists have bred the scent out of such flowers as roses, carnations or sweet peas, but as one breeder said, 'When it comes to new colours, the ayes outvote the noes by two to one'. Fragrant varieties are available, if you ask for them.

Most scented leaves release their perfume only when they are touched, so plant them near paths where you will brush them as you go by.

SCORCH AND SUNBURN

A shade-loving plant like a camellia, a rhododendron or many a palm will get its leaves scorched if it is planted in full sunshine. The bark of trees lives in the shade of their foliage, and if you prune too much foliage away, the bark will get sunburnt, sometimes fatally, the dead bark peeling away and ringbarking the branch. Citrus and avocados are especially susceptible, and after heavy pruning it is traditional to paint the branches with whitewash as a factor 14 sunscreen. Any left-over water-based paint will do at a pinch, if you don't mind a pink or blue lemon tree until the paint wears off.

SETTING OUT
see SPACING OF PLANTS

SHADE

Shade comes in several varieties: the dense summer shade of deciduous trees, the similarly solid shade of buildings, often lightened by reflected light, and the dappled shade from deciduous trees in spring and from eucalypts or the like. **Full shade** implies that the plant is in solid shade all day, probably in a position that isn't open to the sky; **semi-shade** can mean either dappled shade or solid shade for part of the day, as when the plant is growing on, say, the east side of the house so that it gets the morning but not the afternoon sun. (The hot afternoon sun augmented by reflected heat from the walls is less desirable.)

It is sometimes difficult to assess just how shady a spot is; the sun moves around a bit with the seasons, so that a

Shade-loving plants
Camellias
Aucuba japonica
Azaleas
Ferns
Ivy
Hellebores
Violets
Correas
Daphne
Ajuga
Hosta
Lily of the valley
Fuchsias
Japanese maples
Mahonias
Eriostemon
Hydrangeas
Foxgloves
And many, many more!

◀ *There are few flowers that can match trumpet lilies for powerful fragrance. Indeed, a bunch in a small room can be too much of a good thing, and plant breeders have recently been trying to tone it down a bit. Let us hope that they don't go too far.*

▶ *What to do with shade-cloth on a pergola when you want the winter sun? Here is one answer — just roll it over to one side.*

▼ *A shady garden need not be all ferns and greenery. Here lilies flourish in the dappled shade of trees.*

bed that gets full sun in the summer might be in the shade of the house in winter, and a tree might be heavier in foliage than you thought (though you can always thin its branches a little). Try the plant out anyway, and see how it goes; you can always shift it if it is unhappy.

SHADECLOTH

This is a green or black open-weave fabric that is useful for roofing over pergolas and slip-covering greenhouses — and which you can tack over a west-facing window to keep the afternoon sun off if you don't mind its appearance. It serves other uses too; a tent of it can shade a young seedling or

shrub (NEWSPAPER is cheaper) or provide shade for the delicate blossoms of a camellia; stretched between stakes, it will make a temporary windbreak; and it can be laid as a weed-smothering (and expensive) MULCH, under a layer of pebbles for instance, for which it is better than black plastic, as it does allow air to the soil.

It comes in several grades, measured by the percentage of light that it excludes: 80 per cent is pretty generally useful. After a couple of years the plastic from which it is woven degrades with the light, so don't expect it to last forever.

The black usually looks best: like green paint, the green can clash with the greens of foliage. (If you want to make something, be it a stake or a shed, blend in, paint it in the sort of camouflage colours that the army uses: khaki, olive drab, or a cloudy grey, or even black.)

SHADING

Newly set-out plants, be they seedlings or shrubs, often need a bit of temporary shade, which you can provide with a NEWSPAPER or SHADECLOTH tent, or more simply by poking a leafy twig in nearby.

Greenhouses can get awfully hot in summer, and some shading is needed to cool them down. Tomato growers paint the glass with whitewash, often tinted pale green; the rain washes it off by the end of summer. SHADECLOTH looks classier in the garden.

SLIPPERY PAVING

While marble, slate and glazed tiles can look stunning in a formal (and extravagant) garden, their smooth surfaces can be as slippery as glass when they are wet. If you fancy them, make sure they have a textured finish to hold the feet. The same applies, at the other end of the price scale, to pre-cast concrete paving slabs which, cast in steel moulds, can have a dangerously smooth surface. Lay them upside down, using the rougher underside, or better yet, spend the little bit extra for

Slender trees like birches look their best in clumps, planted rather closer than one would normally; but set them at irregular distances or the effect will be artificial.

the 'exposed aggregate' pebbled surface, which looks very much more attractive too.

Bricks, especially, are liable to grow black and slimy algae in damp spots. Clean them up by brushing or even scrubbing with a pale blue copper sulphate solution, bought from the chemist. Bleach can substitute. The effect is temporary, and the cleaning a regular chore.

SNAILS AND SLUGS

'Mrs Snail, Mrs Snail, you leave a pretty silver trail,' the nursery song reminds us, and one way of protecting delicate seedlings from becoming a snail's dinner is to surround them with a protective circle of coarse ashes, on which the snail can't lay its trail of moisture and so reach the plant. (Mr/Mrs would be more apt: slugs and snails can be male or female as the mood takes them.) The standard way of getting rid of these destructive creatures is to sprinkle one of the commercial metaldehyde-based baits, but metaldehyde is poisonous to birds,

which might eat a dying snail. Which is a worry. If you can catch the snail, you can simply squash it; but slugs and snails tend to go out at night, and going out snail-hunting with a flashlight might lead the neighbours into mistaking you for a burglar. Or you can set out saucers of beer, which snails and slugs adore, the idea being that they will fall in and drown.

The garden snail was introduced to Australia to feed English blackbirds, and is the *petit gris* variety on which French gourmets dote. If you fancy a dish of *escargots*, you might try catching a dozen or so, starving them for a few days to make sure they have digested any poisonous plants they might have been eating, and then fattening them up on bran moistened with milk. When they are so fat they can scarcely get back in their shells, it is time to get out the French cookbook.

Here are the white camellia 'Jean Lyne' and its deep pink version 'Edith Linton', growing on the same bush. Quite a conversation piece, but if you don't like the effect, simply trim off the sported shoot.

them (gently!) as though you were playing marbles, and plant them as they have fallen.

In a massed planting of one type of plant — a ground cover or shrubbery, say — there's no need to try for an irregular arrangement. When the plants grow together, their set out on an even grid, square or staggered, won't be obvious.

It's easy to write that one plants, say, petunias 15 centimetres apart or rosebushes a metre each way, but on the ground it's easy to get one's spacing wrong and either run out of plants or have an uneven planting. Tape measures are a nuisance. It's easier to turn a stake or a long handle (a hoe or a rake will serve nicely) into a temporary measuring stick with a few judiciously placed pieces of masking tape or electrician's coloured tape. You can mark your rows by drawing the line with a pointed stake or a hoe; a string line is only worth the bother if it's essential that the line be quite straight, as with the edge of a lawn. Curved lines can be marked out with a hose laid on the ground.

SPACING OF PLANTS

Spacing the plants in a mixed planting calls for nice judgment so that they won't be either standing aloof from each other like ornaments on the mantelpiece or crowding each other out. The latter is the more common problem: the little plants looked so lonely! The basic rule is that you set the plant apart at the same distance as their spread at maturity, and if two plants are of differing spreads, you take the average. Thus, a *Magnolia soulangeana* which might grow 3 metres wide, would be planted 2.5 metres from a camellia with a spread of 2 metres (3+2 =5, divided by 2= 2.5).

A rough plan on paper is a great help in sorting out your spacings, and so is a tape-measure when you come to plant.

Of course, if you want to plant, say, silver birches or eucalypts in a **clump**, you would put them more closely than their normal spread would suggest — they would look best if the spacing were uneven — and let them arrange their branches to suit themselves. Try putting in stakes in the allotted places before you plant to judge the effect; straight lines have a habit of creeping in when you are not looking. Bulbs naturalised in grass or a groundcover look best set out in informal groups, and the old gardener's trick is to scatter

SPORTS

If your white camellia suddenly bears a branch with pink flowers, you have a 'sport', and if you took cuttings from it you'd have a new variety. The change has nothing to do with the activities of bees, but is a mutation, a change in the plant's genes, and its occurrence is purely a matter of chance. Camellias are much given to sporting, but mutations occur in other plants too, though rarely. The growth habit might change (as with the climbing sports of bush roses); the flowers might acquire more petals; or the leaves might be different. Sports are often unstable, and sometimes sport back (revert) to the parent.

Garden safety

Adam, we are told, was a gardener; so we can safely assume that Eve was the first to have to listen to the gardener's lament, 'Oh my aching back!' Aches and pains, to say nothing of more serious injuries, can take all the pleasure out of gardening, but there is no need for them. Haste makes for carelessness and accidents. Relax: Nature doesn't hurry, and there is rarely need for you to.

DRESS FOR THE JOB

Any comfortable old clothes will do. Sturdy shoes or boots of course; good gardening gloves to protect your hands (they are always a bit stiff when they're new, but they soon soften with use), and a hat, or at least a blockout cream — sunburn and the beginnings of skin cancer don't happen only at the beach. Sunglasses offer protection from glare, and also from pokes in the eye. Most insecticides, weedkillers and fungicides are easily absorbed by the skin, so when you're spraying, cover as much skin as possible (a bandana, worn bushranger fashion, makes a good face mask), and change, shower, and wash your clothes when you've finished.

SAVING YOUR BACK

The golden rule to save your back is don't bend your *back*, bend your legs. Don't stoop to the weeding or planting; squat, or kneel down (a folded towel makes a comfortable kneeling pad). And stand up and stretch a bit every quarter of an hour or so, or you'll freeze in position. If you have to

The smart gardener, dressed in comfortable clothes (never mind fashion!), with stout shoes, a hat to keep the sun off, and gloves for protection against scratches. They keep your hands clean, too.

When a rake is laid tines down, you can step on it like this without danger.

Weeding can be tiring. Chinese peasants squat rather than bend over, but most of us will find it easier to kneel on one knee, with a folded towel as a kneeling pad. Get up and stretch every 15 minutes or so.

The right way to pick up a heavy weight — bend your legs, and get as close as you can, even if you do feel a little silly hugging a pot plant!

lift something heavy like a tubbed plant, a rock, or a bag of manure, get as close to it as possible, and bend your legs to get down to where you can get a grip on it. Maybe you can move it by easing it onto an old sugar bag or such and dragging it, but if it proves too heavy, get help. And try not to drop things on your toes or fingers.

UP A TREE

Ladders can be treacherous; if you need to climb one (to clean the house gutters, to prune a tall vine or whatever), make sure it is firmly placed — preferably with someone else to hold it. When you're up there, don't try to reach over further than is safe: move the ladder instead. If you have to climb a tree, say to prune it or to pick fruit, wear non-slip shoes, and make sure you are secure and comfortable before you tackle the job. And don't put your weight on the limb you're about to cut off: that's only funny in Bugs Bunny cartoons. If you need to perform major tree surgery, where you have to climb high or there might be danger from falling branches, it's wisest to call in a professional rather than take risks yourself.

CARE WITH TOOLS

'Beware of the eternal malice of inanimate objects,' Grandma used to say. Garden tools have a habit of causing trouble; don't leave anything lying around where you can trip on it; thrust forks and spades into the ground, and lock secateurs and shears closed so that sharp points and edges are out of the way.

SAFETY WITH THE LAWNMOWER

Lawnmowers need to be treated with special respect. Before you start the mower up, check that the blades are secure — if one flies off, it can amputate your foot — and that the various cables and electrical connections are fixed where they should be. Clear the grass of sticks, stones, toys, the leftovers from last week's barbecue, and of children and pets who might get in harm's way. Don't ever put your hands down near the whirling blades, and keep your feet well away, too. Turn the mower off when you empty the grass catcher, and never go away, even for a minute, and leave the mower running.

IS YOUR GARDEN DESIGNED FOR SAFETY?

If the lawn slopes to a degree where it's difficult to keep the machine completely under control, might it not be better to replace the lawn with groundcover?

Are steps and stairs comfortable in use, provided with handrails where needed, and adequately lit? Do paths and pavings get slippery with algae in wet weather? Washing them down with diluted bleach, copper sulphate, or swimming pool chlorine will remove it.

Is there sufficient room to get past shrubbery, especially pricklies like roses or yuccas? Even unarmed shrubs can poke you in the eye.

Small children can wander into harm's way the minute you turn your back. Are ponds and swimming pools adequately fenced, and will toddlers be tempted to munch on poisonous plants?

NASTIES AND BITIES

For all the trouble Adam and Eve had with the talkative serpent, at least it didn't bite. But the wildlife in our gardens has no such inhibitions; if you suspect you might come across snakes and spiders, keep a watchful eye out. A spider will have trouble biting through a stout glove, but it's better to avoid contact in the first place. Tetanus germs lurk invisibly in compost and manure — are your shots (and the children's) up to date?

CHEMICALS

Ideally, one should buy one's chemicals in small lots as one has need for them, but it's not always convenient or economical to. Sprays, which are needed relatively infrequently, might as well be bought in the smallest packages available. Some don't retain their potency all that long, and it isn't desirable to have more poisons sitting around than one has to. It's a good idea to store them in sealed containers — old jam jars are useful, but label them POISON in case they confuse children — and to keep them in a cool, dark spot in the shed. Inevitably, there'll be some mixed-up spray left over when you've finished spraying. Don't pour it down the drain to pollute the stormwater system; tip it onto a rough patch in the garden to be absorbed, and hopefully biodegraded, by the soil. Empty packets are best buried or put out with the garbage to be buried in the garbage tip; never burn them, or you'll make your incinerator smoke poisonous. Fertiliser is different; it's usually much cheaper to buy the big bag. It doesn't actually go off, but once the bag is opened humidity will make it cake, and breaking up the lumps is a nuisance. You can forestall this by keeping it in sealed containers also: plastic garbage bins, with the tops battened down, will do. Don't bother decanting it, just put the bag and all into the bin, and stick a label on the lid to tell you what's inside. If you find a handful or two left over in the bottom of the bag, it can be sprinkled on the compost heap to enrich it.

And do remember to keep all chemicals out of the reach of children and pets at all times.

Up in a tree or on a ladder, don't try to reach out too far or you are likely to fall. Shift the ladder if you have to.

Tall weak-stemmed flowers like delphiniums look best with a slim cane to each flower spike rather than with the whole plant bundled to a single stout stake.

STAKES AND STAKING

Stakes are used for two purposes: to support young plants (especially trees) until their roots are strong enough to support them, and to hold up plants that would otherwise simply flop, like dahlias, delphiniums, tomatoes and standard roses.

The first use is merely temporary, and once the stake has served its purpose, it should be removed. But how often do we see a tree or shrub which is holding up a long-since superfluous bit of wood? We now know that allowing the tip of the young tree to move a little in the wind is good for it; if you put your tree in bondage like a martyr at the stake it will get lazy and not develop strong roots. All you need to do is to keep it from falling over, and a single loose tie about two-thirds of the way up should be sufficient. String or raffia that will rot in a few months is best — it saves you having to come back and remove it before it starts to strangle the expanding stem. Don't try to straighten out any kinks in the stem; they will disappear as the plant matures.

String is adequate for permanent staking too; long before it rots, you should in any case be checking it and replacing the ties if they get too tight. Admittedly, wire and plastic ties are simpler, and short lengths cut from old nylon stockings do expand a bit, but they look awful.

The stakes themselves can be anything that suits your purpose: lengths of bamboo or cane, or ready-made hardwood stakes (mind the splinters), and can be recycled, if you wish, shortening them if they have rotted in the ground. You sometimes see standard roses tied to pieces of iron pipe, which will at least last the life of the rose, but they aren't pretty and they get awfully hot in the sun. Whatever you choose, let the stake be adequate for its purpose and no more: nothing looks uglier than a forest of mighty timbers holding up slender stems. And consider using two or three smaller stakes for something like a big clump of dahlias rather than trussing everything up to one big one. Ideally, you place the stake only when there is enough growth to hide it, but this can be a bother, to say nothing of skewering delicate roots. A short stake at planting time can always be replaced by a taller one later.

STANDARD

A standard is a shrub or small tree, trained to a single stem to hold its leaves and flowers aloft like a floral lollipop. Standard ROSES have long been familiar, and fuchsias, gardenias, and hibiscus, on stems a metre or so tall, are attractive too. Wisteria, bougainvillea and crepe myrtles can look lovely also, on rather taller stems. A half-standard is just a standard on a shorter than usual stem; the term is mostly used to refer to fruit trees these days.

Roses are not trained from bushes, but BUDDED to a tall understock, and so are weeping cherries and grevilleas. Weeping standard roses — just flexible climbing roses budded to a tall stem — used to be trained over frames like metal crinolines to keep them from just dangling, but these are not easy to come by these days. Such frames would

It isn't difficult to train a standard. Select a young plant with a strong central stem, and tie it to a stake, pinching back the side shoots to channel the plant's energy into the leader. When this is as tall as you want it, you pinch out the tip to encourage the crown of branches. When the crown has developed a little, you can remove the side shoots from the stem to leave it bare. These are lantanas.

One way of getting rid of stink bugs is to suck them off the plant with a vacuum cleaner, emptying the bag into the incinerator.

suit the grevilleas too.

STINK BUGS

Also known as Rutherglen or bronze beetles, these are a pest of citrus trees, eating the young shoots and squirting vile-smelling liquids to protect themselves if they are disturbed. A thorough spray with an insecticide like carbaryl will get rid of them. Or you can, wearing sunglasses to protect your eyes from being squirted, knock them off into a can of kerosene.

SUMMER PRUNING

Though winter is the main pruning season, there are several occasions when you might want to get out your pruning shears in summer:

◆ To prune spring-flowering shrubs like forsythia, weigelas, philadelphus, flowering peaches, and the old-fashioned roses, which bear their flowers on wood made in the previous year. If you cut them in winter, you prune away the embryo flower buds. Prune (if you need to; it isn't obligatory) immediately the flowers are over, by removing the oldest and scruffiest stems. No need to be drastic!

◆ To cut back the long leafy shoots of deciduous fruit trees like apples and pears (also WISTERIA) to three or four leaves, to encourage the plant to put its energy into the short shoots that bear the flowers.

◆ To THIN deciduous trees while they have their foliage and you can see what you are doing.

◆ To shape and control HEDGES and TOPIARY.

See also the special feature on PRUNING.

SUPERPHOSPHATE

More properly called superphosphate of lime, superphosphate is the standard fertiliser for adding PHOSPHORUS to the soil. It contains about 18 per cent of phosphate (phosphorus pentoxide). Despite its title, it isn't alkaline, as the calcium in it is contained mainly as gypsum. Use it sparingly: phosphates are a major cause of water pollution, as 'super'-happy farmers have been finding out in recent years.

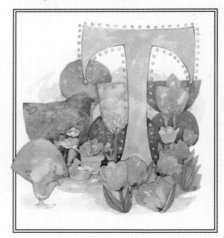

TAP ROOTS

Most trees and shrubs have a main root, the taproot, that grows straight down into the soil to anchor it, the other roots growing out from it. Normally, this comes under the heading of interesting rather than directly useful information, except if you are TRANSPLANTING an established tree and find you have to cut a substantial taproot to do so. Most trees don't take kindly to the shock, and you may well be wise to abandon the attempt.

Sometimes the taproot of a young tree will grow straight down to the bottom of its nursery pot and then coil round and round, a condition which isn't conducive to proper root development when it is planted out. Eucalypts have this habit, and you should always check a young gum tree's roots as you plant it. If there's any sign of coiling, cut off a centimetre or two from the bottom of the root ball with a sharp knife: a new tap root will grow where you cut the old one.

The roots of such vegetables as carrots, radishes and parsnips are tap roots, and if you want them long and straight, you need to dig your soil deeply so that they don't get crooked (and unpleasantly woody) from having to force their way through hard soil. If your soil is shallow or stony, shorter-rooted varieties are the best to choose.

THINNING

Fruit trees, especially apples, pears and stone fruit, often set so many fruit that not only can they not mature them all to full size, but the tree may also decide to take a holiday next year. It is a great help to thin the fruit out when it is big enough to handle — say the size of a ripe cherry. Just pick them off. Usually you would remove about half the fruit in each cluster, or every other one along the stem. You might take a bit more if you want especially large fruit. Don't feel you're depriving yourself, as the total weight of fruit won't be reduced by that much.

Thinning the CROWN of a tree or shrub is a far more effective means of letting in light and air than just cutting it back, after which it will grow back as densely as before. You can do it in the winter, but it's easier to see what you're doing (in a deciduous tree) if you wait until late summer, after growth has stopped. Start by taking out any small, weak branches that crowd the centre, and then remove any that are sitting right over another. This will probably do it, but if you still feel the tree is too dense, you can go further, exercising your artistic judgment. Ideally, when you have finished and cleared up, it shouldn't be obvious that you've been

THINNING

1 *A branch of stone fruit about a third grown and ready for thinning.*

2 *With a third to a half the immature fruit removed, the remainder will grow much bigger, and you'll actually have more to eat — the stones stay the same size!*

there. Don't remove more than about 40 per cent of the foliage, though, and prefer taking a branch right out to cutting it back. You're not trying to make the tree smaller: that's a different job! See also the special feature on PRUNING.

THRIPS

The name has come down to us unchanged from the Ancient Greeks, and is both singular and plural — though you never see a solitary thrips. Not that the insects themselves are easy to see: you have to look very close to see them scurrying around like animated specks of dust. They are summer creatures and eat flowers, making them look as though the petals have been fried, if the blossom opens at all. Roses and dahlias are favourites, especially those of pale colours, and

sometimes they arrive early enough to interfere with the blossoms of fruit trees. But their great love is gladioli, and unless you regularly spray the plants with insecticide from the time their fourth leaf appears, the flowers will be completely ruined. Really bad infestations will leave the leaves looking as though someone has rubbed patches with sandpaper even before the buds appear. Systemic insecticides, such as Rogor, are most effective, but thorough spraying with pyrethrum will clean them

up too — but strike early as the damage they do is irreversible. They are most abundant in hot, dry weather; regular sprinklings will discourage them a little.

TIP PRUNING

This is also known as PINCHING. Sometimes, however, if growth isn't soft enough for your fingers, scissors or secateurs may be called for. You don't normally take off more than a leaf or two with the tip of the shoot.

TOBACCO WATER

An old-fashioned but effective ORGANIC insecticide, particularly good against aphids, tobacco water is made by steeping a couple of large pinches of tobacco or a cigarette or two in a litre of hot water until it is the colour of weak tea, and spraying it on the insects when it is cold. A bit of experimenting will give you the right strength. If you don't smoke you can try making GARLIC water in the same way.

A lavish indulgence in topiary can set the theme for an entire garden. This one is in England, and would look like something out of a fairy-tale on a snowy winter's day.

TOPIARY

You either find the sight of trees and shrubs clipped into geometrical shapes, peacocks, or dinosaurs charming, or you loathe it. But it's easy to do, just needing time and a bit of practice, and a grevillea peacock presiding over a cottage garden mix of flowers would be a great conversation piece.

Yew, box and bay are the traditional plants, but you can use any fine-leafed plant that will take the constant clipping (see HEDGES). Privet is a possibility; *Grevillea rosmarinifolia* and its hybrids grow fast enough for the impatient, though they aren't very long-lived; and the Japanese shear Kurume azaleas into shapes and a use a technique known as 'cloud PRUNING'.

If you are planning something like a dragon sitting on a pedestal, it's best to have two plants, one for the dragon and one for the pedestal. Proceed as though you were making a HEDGE, cutting the young plants back to keep them bushy or they'll be thin and flimsy looking. Some support in the early stages will be useful. For a simple shape like an obelisk, a single stake will be enough; for anything fancier, you need a temporary frame to train your branches to. This might be improvised simply from a few battens nailed together, or you could make — and can sometimes buy — a complete form made of heavy galvanised wire.

A tree or shrub clipped into topiary is looked after just as though it were part of a hedge, though you will probably want to be a bit more meticulous with your clipping. As with any shrub, water and fertiliser will be called for from time to time.

A wire frame made in the shape of a sphere, pyramid or what have you can be covered with a small-leafed ivy or creeping fig for a 'mock-topiary', which is easier and faster. The creeper will need trimming to keep the shape precise.

TRACE ELEMENTS

Apart from the big three — NITROGEN, PHOSPHORUS, and POTASSIUM — plants need quite a few elements to build their tissues: magnesium, iron, boron, manganese, calcium, and about twenty others. But they aren't needed in any quantity — hence the term trace elements — and a half-way decent soil should supply them. A deficiency of each has its own symptoms (the characteristic between-the-veins yellowing of leaves due to shortage of manganese for instance), but if you suspect a trace element deficiency, it is easiest to simply add a fertiliser containing them all. Check the package: not all 'complete' fertilisers contain trace elements. If the bag doesn't say 'contains trace elements', check the analysis on the back. If you just add one, you can upset the balance of the soil and create a shortage of others, merely escalating the problem and ending up with a stack of half-used fertiliser bags.

Australian soils are often deficient in boron, which manifests itself in plants that just don't seem to want to grow; a light sprinkling of household borax can be the answer — but see above.

TRANSPLANTING

Shifting established trees and shrubs around like so much furniture can be pretty impressive, though it isn't the sort of job one undertakes lightly. Not all plants take kindly to the shock: rhododendrons, azaleas and camellias, with their fibrous root systems, move easily; magnolias and most Australian natives have rather sparse and thongy roots and are just about impossible to move. (If in doubt, it's better to leave a choice plant where it is and rearrange your other plantings around it.) The younger and smaller any plant is, the greater your chances of success will be, and it is always a wise precaution to take some cuttings in case you lose your old plant.

The best time for shifting anything is during its dormancy, which usually means in the winter. Only in the greatest emergency should you try to

TRANSPLANTING AN ESTABLISHED
TREE OR SHRUB

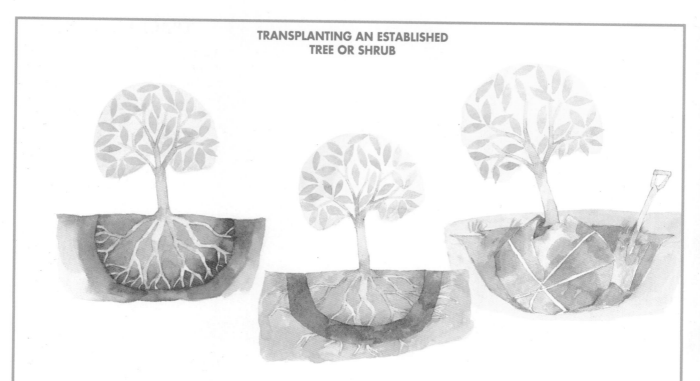

1 *Well ahead of time, cut around the roots with a sharp spade in a circle about 40 to 60 cm across (depending on the size of the tree), filling in the trench you make with fine-textured soil.*

2 *A mat of fine roots will grow into the new soil and help hold everything together.*

3 *When the big day arrives, dig around to expose the root ball, bundling it up in hessian as you go.*

4 *Make the planting hole in the new spot wider than you need,.*

5 *Place the tree in its new home, making sure it sits no deeper than before.*

6 *Fill up the hole with soil, gently treading it into place, and then water thoroughly.*

Tulip bulbs are not cheap, so a massed display like this is a great extravagance. But don't they look wonderful?

Three guy ropes give a young tree better support than a single stake: but pad their attachment to the tree, or the bark will be bruised.

move an established plant in the summer, and never, *never*, while it is actually making new growth. As far ahead as possible — preferably the previous winter — you should prune the roots, undercutting as deeply as possible (see ROOT PRUNING), so as to reduce the root ball to about 60 per cent of the diameter of the spread of the branches. The new roots growing from the cuts will form a compact mass around the edges and help hold the whole thing together. Mark where you've cut with some string, or a circle of pebbles, so that when you come to lift the plant you know where to dig. A day or two before the operation, water thoroughly, and make sure the new spot is ready. You may also want to cut the branches back a bit, to balance the inevitable loss of roots.

Then it is a matter of digging gently to free the root ball from the surrounding soil. As you go, wrap it tightly with hessian and string, lest it fall apart. Then lift it out, cradling it from beneath. This is the tricky part, for you don't want the soil to fall off the roots, and the whole thing is

enormously heavy. Carry the plant gently to its new position, set it in the hole you have just dug to receive it (it's a lot easier to manoeuvre if this is wider than strictly necessary), and set the plant in place, making sure it ends up no deeper than before. Some support will be needed, and three guy ropes are better than a stake, especially for a tree. Leave them in place for a year. Several sets of strong hands will be called for, and beer or coffee all round at the end of the operation will probably be in order. If you are shifting only a fairly small shrub, the job is easier and you can dispense with the preliminary root pruning, just taking as big a root ball as possible.

For the first year or even two, the transplanted plant will need to be treated as a convalescent, making sure above all that it is never allowed to dry out. It may also be a good idea to rig up SHADECLOTH protection against drying winds and hot sun. Don't be surprised if the tree refuses to flower until it's established again. Some people remove flowers if they appear, to conserve the plant's strength.

The large trees that landscape contractors buy from specialist nurseries are available to the public too, but their installation is really best left to a professional, and the choice of species is apt to be limited to those that do transplant reliably. Many of the tree nurseries will plant for you, or at least recommend a contractor who can. A 5 metre tree, so installed, is an expensive item, but the instant maturity that it can bring to a new garden can make the cost worthwhile.

TULIPS

The most gorgeous of the spring BULBS, tulips refuse to flower unless they get a cold and frosty winter first. In a mild climate, it's possible to fool them by buying the bulbs early and putting them in the vegetable drawer of the refrigerator for at least six weeks (labelled if the cook will mistake them for vegetables) and then planting them as late as you dare, once the weather has cooled down: the end of May or even the first week in June in most parts of Australia. Keep them lavishly watered from the time they come up, to keep them cool. (The bed will need to be perfectly drained.) If the flower buds shrivel as they appear, your soil just wasn't cool enough. You can rarely repeat the trick: in winterless climates, tulips, crocuses, some of the more exotic alliums, and the crown imperial are best thought of as expensive annuals and pot plants. Console yourself with the beautiful warm-climate bulbs: hippeastrums, freesias, sparaxis and the fragrant *Hymenocallis*, the sacred lily of the Incas. Daffodils and Dutch irises are in between; they need less cold than tulips, but in subtropical climates they appreciate the refrigerator treatment.

Striped tulips are the result of a VIRUS, which is spread by APHIDS; it is a matter of taste whether you throw them out or admire them.

In these days of high costs, many nurseries are being forced to pare down their lists to the best-sellers. So beauties like the Higo camellias (this one is 'Kakehashi') remain rare.

UNDERSTOCKS

Despite the stories about the winegrower who grafted white grapes onto red vines and could only make rosé wine, the understock doesn't affect the plant grafted onto it that much — which is perhaps just as well, as in Australia we aren't offered the wide choice of understocks for grafted plants that is customary in Europe. There one might buy the same variety of apple budded on EM III, IV, or IX, which are apple cultivars selected (by the East Malling Research Station in Norfolk, hence EM) for the different sizes of the resulting trees. EM IX is a very weak grower indeed, so that the tree dependent on the vigour of its roots doesn't grow to much more than shrub size.

But this is exceptional: usually the whole point of grafting is to lend the cultivated scion the strength of wild roots. Thus the cultivars of *Camellia reticulata* are grafted to the much stronger growing *C. sasanqua*, and lilac to privet. Privet is indeed too strong for the lilac, and will try to shake it off its back, so you plant with the graft as deep as you can so that the lilac will (eventually) make roots of its own and smother the privet. Roses are budded onto various wild and cultivated roots, and a rose grower will choose the local favourite, in New South Wales and much of the United States, the thornless *Rosa multiflora*; in England, the very cold-tolerant *Rosa canina*, the dog rose; in Western Australia, *R. fortuneata* is favoured for its ability to grow in sandy soils. Citrus are often budded on seedling lemons, but if you are planning to plant them in cool climates, you would be wise to ask for them on 'trifoliata' stock (*Poncirus trifoliata*), which lends the plant its ability to cope with greater cold than it would have on its own roots. In this matter (as in so much!) the advice of your local nursery is invaluable.

UNUSUAL PLANTS

It's always interesting to have something a bit different in the garden, whether it be an uncommon variety of a common plant or one that is unusual in its own right. But a garden containing little else can easily become a horticultural zoo — or worse, a horticultural hospital. Don't make the mistake of equating rarity and difficulty with beauty: the popular plants are that precisely because they are beautiful and simple to grow.

Mail-order nurseries are often the most fruitful source of unusual plants. Look for them in the advertisements in gardening magazines. See BUYING PLANTS BY MAIL.

A collection of variegated plants at the Chelsea Flower Show in London. In the garden, a group like this would look best with a plain backdrop of green leaves and grass.

VARIEGATED LEAVES

Patterns of yellow, white or even pink on the basic green of leaves can be very pretty, and many common plants have variegated forms. But variegated plants are apt to clash with each other, and you need to use them with discretion, or the result can be gaudy and artificial, rather like a room with a different wallpaper on each wall.

The variegation reduces the amount of the CHLOROPHYLL–bearing area of the leaves, and variegated plants are rarely as vigorous as their plain green counterparts; often they are shy with their flowers too. Many have arisen as SPORTS and tend to revert to plain green: if you see a green shoot, remove it at once or it will quickly take over.

White-patterned plants especially are apt to be scorched in full sun; take the hint and use them to bring light to shaded places.

VERSAILLES TUB

The ornamented, square wooden tubs originally designed for Louis XIV's orange trees at Versailles can add a pleasing note of formality to a more

no

modest garden. They usually have a removable bottom, to make it easy to take the tree out in order to prune its roots. (You just lift the whole thing by its handles onto a suitable box or such, and the sides drop down. Practical people, the French.) By all means call yours a caisse de Versailles, and plant in it whatever you fancy. A camellia or hibiscus would look nice; so would a clump of agapanthus or cannas. Oranges are not obligatory.

VIREYA

A name we will be hearing much more of in the future, *Vireya* is one of the sections into which the huge genus *Rhododendron* is divided. But while the rhododendrons proper are plants for cool, moist climates, the vireyas (or vireya azaleas: azaleas are a rhododendron subgroup also) are subtropical beauties, coming mainly from the highlands of New Guinea. The

only Australian rhododendron, *R. lochae* from north Queensland, is a member of the group. Vireyas resemble the common evergreen azaleas, except that their leaves are dark and glossy, and they bear ultra-glamorous flowers in shades of salmon, red, yellow and apricot; some are deliciously fragrant. Most look to be about rosebush-sized in growth. They don't seem prone to botrytis, which rots the flowers of the Indian azaleas in humid climates, and some bloom right through the summer. They are still new to gardens, and not easy to propagate, so they are still quite expensive to buy, but they promise to be easy to grow, in the half-shade and in the acid, well-watered but well-drained soil that ordinary azaleas like.

VIRUSES

In plants as in humans, virus diseases are mostly incurable, and distressingly common. Some, like rose wilt, tobacco

Versailles tubs at the Chateau de Malmaison near Paris, each housing an immaculate standard bay tree. Despite their size, they are easily moved around.

Like this one, many vireya rhododendrons are sold unnamed, but all are lovely.

mosaic virus (which affects tobacco's cousin the tomato) and the red-core of strawberries, are crippling, if not fatal; others seem to just reduce the vigour of the plant a bit, and you don't really notice until you compare the health of a virus-free strain. Sometimes the virus makes its presence evident by an unnatural pallor or mottling of the leaves. If virus-free stock of such plants as strawberries, lilies, and daphne is available, it is well worth paying extra for. Only in one case is a virus thought desirable: the one that makes tulips 'break' into stripes, though striped tulips are much less popular than they used to be.

Virus diseases are spread by APHIDS and by poor garden hygiene; don't use the same secateurs on healthy plants as on any that you think might have a virus, unless you first sterilise them by dipping them in undiluted bleach. And don't propagate by cuttings or division from virus-infected plants if you can avoid it. If a plant does develop a crippling virus, there is nothing to do but destroy it before it can infect others. Happily, viruses are rarely transmitted through seed. If a favourite lily for instance, should succumb to virus, you can often save your stock by saving seeds and growing them.

It is the worry about introducing unsuspected viruses (as well as more obvious pests and diseases) that leads countries to maintain quarantine laws.

WATER GARDENS

Few things are prettier than a garden pond, with sparkling goldfish swimming about beneath the water lilies and water-loving plants flourishing at the margins — but a badly made and managed pond can easily become a muddy, mosquito-infested swamp.

The first essential is to site your pond in the sun; shade will spoil the reflections off the water; algae will flourish and make it turgid; and the water lilies won't flower.

Then, it needs to be given a properly watertight lining, whether of concrete, PVC or, easiest of all, one of the pre-formed fibreglass pond liners you can buy in a variety of shapes and sizes. Try to allow a place where the pool can overflow without creating a disaster; fill it with water and you are in business.

Then you should have fish to eat the mosquito lavae, and they will need submerged and floating water plants to ensure oxygen in the water. You can usually get these at an aquarium shop, and all you have to do is put them in the water.

Most people find waterlilies essential in a water garden, and they are easy. In winter or early spring, plant a lily or two in a box or large pot full of the richest soil and just put it in the pond. As long as they have 25 to 35 centimetres of water over their roots they will flourish.

The shimmer of light on water is beautiful in itself, and there's no need to fill your pond with waterlilies and their kind — it is a good rule to cover no more than a third of the surface with foliage. Almost unplanted, this pool gives the impression of a waterhole in a rainforest.

Winning the war against weeds

What a year it has been for weeds! But then it always is — they are one of those things, like death and taxes, that are always with us. Console yourself with the thought that if your soil can't grow a decent crop of weeds, then it won't be able to grow anything else either.

BUT WHAT IS A WEED?

A weed has been described as a plant out of place, and that is true. A weed is a plant that insists on growing where you don't want it. It may be desirable somewhere else: like couch grass, which is a very good grass in most lawns, but a terrible pest if it gets into a flower bed (which it will do if you don't keep your EDGES trimmed); the much-hated cape tulip (*Homeria elegans*), which is a gorgeous flower despite its habit of seeding itself everywhere and poisoning horses and cattle if it gets into paddocks; or privet, a serviceable hedge but apt to come up everywhere, with a special fondness for rainforest gullies where it quickly shades out the native vegetation. Or your own pet hate, which is almost certainly a foreign plant that someone has regarded sufficiently highly to introduce it to your district from a homeland where it behaves itself.

WHY GET RID OF WEEDS?

In the first place, because they blur and spoil the picture you are trying to create with your plants; clearing out the interlopers and restoring the picture is one of gardening's most satisfying jobs. But more because they compete with your chosen plants for space, light and air, and, especially, for water. And in bushland they reproduce faster than the native plants that have legitimate possession, so that they die out. No one who has the privilege of living near natural country could be so unthinking as to allow their garden to be the headquarters from which the weeds can invade and destroy it, surely? (And yet people do; they will insist on growing such INVASIVE things as privet and pampas grass, heedless of the consequences.)

Weeds, like desirable plants, can be annuals or perennials; they might even be shrubs or vines. The easiest to deal with are the annuals, like chickweed, the petty spurge (*Euphorbia peplus*) and the winter (*Poa*) and summer (*Digitaria*) grasses. You just pull them out and throw them on the compost heap; they are rarely so substantial that this is heavy work. But do it before they go to seed. Weed seeds are long-lived, and there is truth in the old saying that one year's seeding means seven years weeding. If you find a few

Despite its peculiar smell, crofton weed is rather pretty (it comes in pink, too); but it is dangerous to horses, which, unaware that it is poisonous, like to eat it.

Aboriginal people called the blackberry 'the white man's footprint'. These are thornless blackberries, grown for their fruit, but their owner would be wise to keep a sharp eye out for any attempts to escape.

The petty spurge (Euphorbia peplus) is an annual, and easy enough to get rid of. It is often covered in rust, but doesn't seem to be able to pass it on to garden plants.

The ornamental lantanas are safe to grow, but the wild one is a terrible pest in rainforests. It pulls up easily, but you have to return to remove the crop of seedlings that will come up in a few weeks.

but even if you do, don't be surprised to find a crop of seedlings later. Don't put perennial weeds on the compost heap; burn them (if that is allowed in your area) and use the ash used to restore some of the nutrients they have robbed from the soil, or take to the tip.

Weedkillers can be useful with perennial weeds, but it is dangerous just to spray them on indiscriminately. Not only are they poisonous, there is also a risk of the spray drifting on to plants you want unharmed. (Don't ever spray anything on a windy day!) It is better to dig out what you can, and then just touch any regrowth with the poison. GLYCOPHOSATE ('Zero', 'Roundup') is the safest, as it won't poison the soil; wildly toxic substances like dalapon, 2.4D and sodium chlorate are dangerous pollutants and are best left to professionals. At one time, small flame-throwers were favoured, but their main use is to make you feel like Rambo; the risk of setting the whole garden on fire is very real.

If you can prevent weeds from establishing themselves in the first place, the war is half won. Nature leaves no bit of

Paspalum is a coarse grass that shouldn't be allowed to get a footing in the lawn — it grows faster than the good grass, forcing you to mow more often.

Allium triquetrum, the angled onion, is one of those weeds that is actually quite pretty — but allow it to get established and it will take over the garden.

Farmers regard thistles as a sign of fertile land, which is some consolation if you're struggling to pull the prickly so-and-sos out! Glyphosate kills them quickly.

Pull out all the tap root, to prevent regrowth, of flatweed (above) or dandelion. Flatweed has several small flowers on each stem, the dandelion only one.

coming up, give that area a thorough watering to encourage their friends to appear so that you can deal with them all at once. And it's easier to pull them up when the soil is comfortably moist. Hoeing will often dig small weed plants out en masse, and you can use a trowel or hand fork, if they are larger, to make sure you get every bit. The fork is better where there are BULBS hiding below the surface; a trowel might cut them in half by mistake.

Perennial weeds are much tougher cookies: most have substantial bits underground, like the bulbs of OXALIS or ONION WEED, the taproots of dandelions or the runners of couch or KIKUYU, from which they can regenerate, and you have to get every bit of these out. This usually means digging rather than pulling, sometimes with a full-size border fork, and then getting down on your knees again to sift out the fine bits. The same goes for shrubs like privet, lantana and blackberries, most of which can regrow from quite small pieces of root; you need to get rid of *everything*,

ground unoccupied: in native bush either there is a plant growing there, or the bare soil is covered with a natural MULCH. This is what she likes, and if you leave unoccupied soil in the garden, she will fill it up — with plants in the wrong place, what you call weeds. Copy Nature's approach, setting your plants close enough that they shade out any weeds that try to come up (you can fill in among shrubs with GROUNDCOVERS, and keep your lawn growing strongly enough that the grass keeps a tight cover) and mulching any areas where lowly foliage isn't appropriate, like beds of annuals, perennial borders or the vegetable plot. But don't try to mulch on top of established weeds, annual or perennial, because they'll just come through and you'll wish you had got rid of them first.

And before you pull out a plant, make sure it is a weed! Sometimes garden plants will self-sow, and if you think the little plant looks like something desirable, leave it until it has identified itself.

WATERSHOOTS

A watershoot, growing rapidly from the base of a rosebush and crowned with a candelabrum of flowers.

Watershoots on a fruit tree will develop into new branches. If these are desirable, retain them; if not, remove them before they take too much of the plant's energy.

WATERSHOOTS

The soft, sappy and rapid-growing shoots that come from low down on the plant can be a nuisance on fruit trees, as if you allow them to develop, they may clog up the open framework that you have been carefully pruning the tree to maintain. Break them off as they arise, unless they are useful to you. On shrubs like mock oranges, forsythias, and especially roses, watershoots are the plant's way of keeping themselves young, and so they should be cherished. At the appropriate pruning time, you might remove one or more of the oldest branches to make way for the new ones.

WHITE GARDENS

All-white gardens are fashionable at the moment, and they can look lovely and cool in the hottest weather. But such a severely limited colour scheme calls for extra attention to the greens and greys of the accompanying foliage, and to the forms and textures of your plants. And to the whites themselves: white flowers aren't uniform in colour. Some, like camellias and candytuft, are indeed laundry-white; others have shadings of

All-white plantings look cool and refreshing in the heat — but don't forget they are actually white and green!

White Flowers

Magnolias (also pink)
Camellias (also pink and red)
Gardenias
Roses (also most other colours)
Lilies (also red, pink, yellow, orange)
Tobacco flowers (also pink and red)
Agapanthus (also blue)
Snow in summer (*Cerastium*)
Petunias (also blue, pink, red)
Irises (also most other colours)
Jasmine
Azaleas (also red and pink)

green (like snapdragons and some lilies), palest pink (as in many roses and magnolias), or cream (like stocks, white zinnias and yucca), and the stark whites can make these look dirty by contrast.

Take care with white as a blending colour; things like white primulas are so dazzling they can shout down the flowers they are meant to be setting off.

WILTING

If a plant wilts, ninety-nine times out of a hundred it is simply thirsty, and should recover quickly if it is watered without delay. Some plants like hydrangeas and silver beet are notoriously thirsty and will droop on a hot day even when the soil is moist enough for their neighbours. If the plant doesn't recover, then you may be faced with a VIRUS disease, like wilt of roses, spotted wilt of tomatoes, or broad bean wilt, which also affects sweet peas; or with a FUNGUS usually infecting the plant at ground level, like clematis wilt or the collar rot that attacks delphiniums and the cabbage tribe. Wilt diseases are not very common, fortunately, as there is little you can do about them, except remove the wilted plant in order to keep the infection from spreading.

WISTERIA

Both the Chinese wisteria (*Wisteria sinensis*) and the Japanese (*W. floribunda*) with its long trails of flowers, are very vigorous vines indeed, and they

Wisteria is naturally an enormous vine, but with careful pruning you can tailor it to fit a modest support like this arch.

need regular pruning to keep them to an appropriate size for most garden situations. Happily, they don't mind it at all. The Japanese even use them for BONSAI and they still flower delightfully. Train them from youth, selecting the few main shoots you need to cover the wall or pergola and cutting out others, so that there won't be a tangle of growth. Once the plant has filled its allotted space, it is pruned in summer, by cutting back the long bare shoots that appear when

flowering is over, to three or four leaves. The result will be a lot of short twigs which will bear an abundance of flowers, and a plant that looks handsome even in winter. Cutting back hard in winter will lead to much long growth and few flowers. Watch out for the long runners that come from the base in summer; they will take root and make a nuisance of themselves. Cut them out completely when you notice them.

The velvety beige seed pods are decorative in winter, but the seeds they contain are poisonous. Don't let them develop if they might pose a risk to children.

After it flowers, wisteria makes long whippy shoots. Trim these back to two or three leaves in summer, and you not only control the plant's growth, you also encourage more flowers.

The rose 'Queen Elizabeth', the child of two very different parents, exhibits enormous hybrid vigour, often growing 3 metres tall.

XENIA

When two plants are hybridised, the resulting offspring are often more strong-growing than their parents. An example is the enormously strong-growing 'Queen Elizabeth' rose, the child of two very distantly related roses. This **hybrid vigour** (xenia is the technical term) is exploited by the breeders of F1 HYBRIDS, but it tends to disappear in later generations, and very highly bred plants, like some roses and orchids, can end up being weak and sickly. It is one of Nature's ways of keeping species pure.

XEROPHYTE

Xerophytes (the word is bastard Greek) are plants that are adapted to living in arid climates. They are valuable in gardens for their drought resistance, which is not to say that they don't earn their place for their beauty. Xerophytes often have a distinct character of their own and need to be placed with care among other plants, both so that the combinations don't look ridiculous (imagine an azalea and a cactus together!) and to ensure that they don't get distressed by too much watering.

Cacti and succulents are the obvious examples, and the hard leaves of so many Australian plants are designed to conserve moisture too.

YELLOW

There are fashions in horticulture as in most human activities, and currently yellow flowers are unfashionable. Gaudy, the gardening trendies call them. True, this is the colour to which the human eye is most sensitive, so it does tend to leap out from its surroundings and dominate a colour scheme. But it is a bright and cheerful colour, effective in our strong sunshine, which can make delicate tones look wishy-washy. If you don't like bright yellow, there are flowers in soft yellow: many roses, some irises, evening primroses. Yellow (usually sold as 'Golden') leaved conifers are another matter. Our strong sun brightens the colour, and they do look brassy. Leave them to the English, with their pale sunlight.

YOUNG PEOPLE'S GARDENS

Small children can enjoy anything, and can have great fun with a patch of ground in which to plant fast-growing flowers and vegetables like nasturtiums, sunflowers or lettuces, even miniature roses. But as they grow into adolescence they are apt to find the whole activity either childish or only suitable for their dotty, old-fashioned parents. Don't try to force gardening on them if they find it boring. Soon they will have homes of their own, and may well find they have inherited your love of gardens.

YUCCA

Handsome evergreen perennials from North America, admired for their bold, architectural form, columns of creamy white flowers in summer, and their great tolerance of drought and neglect. But each of those sturdy leaves ends in a sharp spike, which makes them hazardous to anyone who approaches them. Plant them safely out of the way, and never where they might encroach on the public footpath — you will be held liable if a passerby is injured. The same goes for other thornies like climbing roses and bougainvillea: don't plant them on the front fence.

Yellow may be out of fashion, but what could look more cheerful in the spring sunshine than this bed of golden ranunculi and alyssum?

The Joys of Exhibiting

Lady at a flower show: 'Fancy giving *that* a prize! Why, *I* have better gladioli (or roses, or onions or whatever) in my own garden!' Vicar to lady: 'Well, Madam, why didn't you bring them along, and then we could have given *you* the prize?'

And why not, indeed? There do seem to be fewer flower shows than there used to be (perhaps it is something to do with the rise of television and the decline of vicars) but they are one of the most civilised sports that has ever been devised, and a great way of meeting people and sharing the pleasures of gardening. And it is still a thrill to win a prize.

BE PREPARED

If you fancy the idea of taking part, first go and see a couple of shows. The local garden club can tell you when and where they are held, and they are usually advertised in the local paper. Shows are always a pleasure to see, and you can get an idea of what sort of thing wins prizes — and what you might like to try showing. Take a copy of the show schedule in hand: comparing its wording with the prize-winners on the bench can be enlightening. You might even like to think of joining the club that runs the show. They often have talks and demonstrations for what are still quaintly called 'novice exhibitors', and often there will be classes at the show that are restricted to members only.

CHOOSE PRIZE-WINNING VARIETIES

Concentrate on growing your own favourites; you'll be willing to give them that little bit of extra love and attention that wins prizes. Grow them as well as you can, not stinting on manure and water, and keeping pests and diseases at bay. With the more highly developed flowers, like roses, dahlias, chrysanthemums or gerberas, it's worth growing the varieties that conform best to show standards, the exhibition varieties that produce the largest and most perfectly formed flowers. With vegetables, this is essential: part of the competition with tomatoes or onions is having specimens bigger and rounder than the other fellow's.

These exhibition varieties are not always the best for a garden display: they might be shy with their flowers, more prone to pests or diseases than most people would be prepared to put up with, or just plain cantankerous, the breeder having sacrificed the vigour of the plant to the perfect blooms. You can expect the judges to be familiar with this, and to take into account the skill needed to bring a difficult variety to perfection, but happily there is usually a choice of varieties that are both garden and show worthy. Chances are, you have some in your garden already. In making your choice, the advice of the show buffs at the garden club is invaluable. One thing they will tell you, and which most beginners ignore, is that it's usually best to have more than one plant of each variety, because it increases your chances of having that perfect bloom on the day.

Being naturally short-stemmed, camellias are shown with just two leaves attached, and placed on the bench, but they bruise easily and need careful handling. They will last the day if they are spayed with water. This is a prizewinner, 'Giulio Nuccio Variegated'.

A fine show of perfect flowers of the cactus dahlia 'Alloway Cottage'. Just the thing to gladden the heart on show day!

GOING TO THE SHOW

At your first show, it may be wise to avoid the specialist flowers altogether, and enter a class such as most general flower shows have for something like 'three stems of a flowering shrub' or 'one stem of a herbaceous perennial', which allows you at least to bring something you actually have in the garden. Don't feel that this is beneath you — the competition in these classes can be just as fierce as among the rose-aholics! Get a copy of the schedule from the show secretary as far in advance as possible, and make sure you understand it — schedules are often full of jargon. You might find the class calls for, say, 'three exhibition roses, distinct', which means they *must* be different varieties — three different reds would be acceptable, but you'd probably get more points for a red, a pink and a yellow — 'not

Dahlia shows are held in autumn, at the end of the season when the cool weather gives better flowers, and dahlia fanciers propagate their plants from cuttings to delay flowering. It's easy to do.

Plant clumps of tubers in October or early November in a box of potting soil. When the shoots have two or three sets of leaves, detach them to use as cuttings. (The tubers will usually give two or even three batches, and are then discarded.)

Break the shoots off gently, trim them with a razor blade, and insert them at once in sandy soil, either one to a pot or in twos and threes. But don't mix your varieties up! The new plants should be ready to plant out about Christmas time.

necessarily distinct' or 'NND' means you could have more than one specimen of one of your chosen varieties. Similarly, 'double' or 'single' may have a specific meaning with a particular flower, as with camellias. A well-written schedule should explain what it means, but don't hesitate to ask: it's embarrassing for the garden club too if an exhibit has to be disqualified as 'NAS', or 'not according to schedule'. At this stage, you'll probably feel ambitious, but don't enter too many classes; it takes time to get your flowers ready, and you won't have much time between when the hall opens and the judging begins. Three or four entries will be plenty.

With vegetables, make sure you know how the points will be awarded. The commonly used pointing system devised by the Royal Horticultural Society in London takes difficulty of culture into account, so that a cabbage, say, can only get a maximum of 15 points out of 20, no matter how perfect; while an exhibition onion can get the full 20 — and don't giggle, it's extremely difficult to grow a huge onion to perfect, unblemished symmetry. Don't load your exhibit with too many of the low-pointed varieties.

HOW TO WIN — OR AT LEAST MAKE A NICE DISPLAY

With any flower, freshness is all important: no insect bites, bruised petals, no evident discoloration from too long a time in the vase. Then, you want to show it at the most beautiful stage of its development. A rose is shown fully expanded but before the centre has parted to reveal the stamens; a spray of lilac when about three-quarters of the flowers have opened but there are still buds to set them off; a gladiolus should have as many blooms open as possible, though none fading

Nurserymen often bring their newest varieties to the major flower shows to introduce them to the public, usually mounting great displays like this.

yet, and so on. Vegetables should be mouth-wateringly fresh and unblemished, but you are usually allowed to trim the leaves of vegetables such as cauliflowers and broccoli. A look at some prize winners will show you what is expected. Don't be put off; showing isn't difficult — I won my first best-in-show as a dumb fourteen-year-old.

Cut flowers in the cool of the evening before the show, trim any untidy leaves (if you can do it so that no one notices), and stand them in deep water overnight, wrapping each bloom in tissue paper if need be so that they don't bump against each other. If you can carry them to the show in water, it's best to do so, but if not, gently wrap them and lay them across the back seat of the car. Show organisers usually supply vases but you'll probably need to bring butcher's paper to crumple into the mouth of the vase to hold the blooms in place. Take secateurs, a fine-pointed pair of scissors for trimming, and a soft watercolour brush (a number 6 sable if you can afford it) to wipe off any bugs and dust. Drive carefully, so as to jostle neither the flowers nor your pre-show nerves.

When you arrive, get your vases and entry cards from the secretary, and start to put your flowers in the vases, making sure that they stand up to face the judge (that's what the crumpled paper is for), and that if there is more than one (usually three) in the vase, they are gracefully arranged (you get points for arrangement). It's a courtesy to those who will admire your exhibit to label each variety with its name, and some shows insist on it. Be prepared to be pleasantly surprised by the helpfulness of your rivals, but don't bother them with questions. And good luck! Even if you don't win best in show, you'll have had a great time.

ZYGOMORPHIC

A flower so described has, not the radial (actinomorphic) symmetry of the rose, but the bilateral symmetry displayed by the human body. Orchids and pansies are examples.

The distinction is of great importance in classifying plants, and is the reason why the 'geraniums' of gardens are not classed with the closely related true geraniums but in a genus of their own, *Pelargonium*. Plant breeders have succeeded in making 'geraniums' almost completely round, but if you look carefully, you can see that the petals are not disposed quite evenly about the centre.

▲ *The bloody cranesbill, Geranium sanguineum, with the completely symmetrical flowers that distinguish the true geraniums from their relatives the pelargoniums.*

▼ *Pansies, with their zygomorphic flowers, in which children have always seen smiling faces.*

▶ *This mixed border, with its plants of varying weights, and harmonising pink and white flowers, is characteristic of the cottage garden style.*

The new 'Mikado' bears the sort of huge, perfectly formed flowers rose judges swoon over. It's a reliable grower, too.

ABOUT THE AUTHOR

Roger Mann B.Arch, ARAIA, AAILA is a landscape architect and freelance writer. He has designed gardens in three states and the ACT, has lectured in landscape architecture at the University of Adelaide and for the Centre for Continuing Education at the Australian National University, and has been Gardening Editor for *Family Circle* (under the nom-de-plume Roger Griffin) and *NOW* magazine. A keen gardener since the age of ten, Roger currently lives and practises in Sydney, where he is making a new garden for himself and learning to play the harpsichord.

Published by Murdoch Books, a division of Murdoch Magazines Pty Ltd, 213 Miller Street, North Sydney NSW 2060

Photography: Stirling Macoboy, Geoffrey Burnie, Denise Greig, Roger Mann, Better Homes and Gardens, Lorna Rose
Cover photograph: Jerry Harpur/Auscape
Design: Di Quick
Illustrations: Helen McCosker
Picture Research: Dianne Bedford

Publisher: Anne Wilson
Publishing Manager: Mark Newman
Production Manager: Catie Ziller
Marketing Manager: Mark Smith
National Sales Manager: Keith Watson

National Library of Australia
Cataloguing-in-Publication Data
Mann, Roger, 1948– .
The secrets of good gardening: an A–Z guide.
ISBN 0 86411 313 7.
1. Gardening. I. Title.
635